Quilt Blocks and Quilts from your Favorite Fabrics

Recycling Fabrics as You Learn to Quilt

Creative Publishing
international

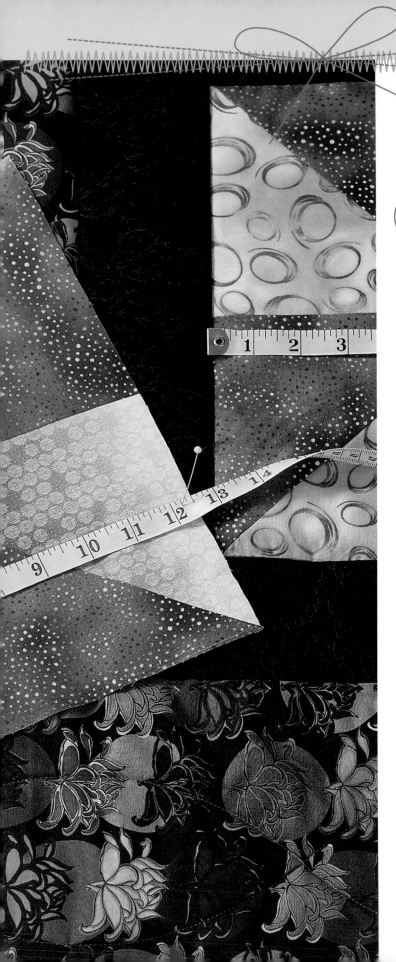

contents

welcome to quilting!

To create a quilt, you follow a simple, step-by-step process. It's a lot like putting together a jigsaw puzzle! In this book, you'll learn how to make a dozen simple block projects and three quilt-sampler projects, working with three quiltmaking techniques: patchwork piecing, working with foundation materials, and appliqué. Each project teaches you a different way to put the blocks together (known as setting) and you'll learn how to finish them, too. You'll stitch everything on the sewing machine, so you'll be done in no time!

Work with colorful cotton fabrics—or with fabrics harvested from shirts, ties, T-shirts, and jeans. While you're digging in the closet, you might also want to pull out old bridesmaid or prom dresses, vintage linens, and trims. You can turn these one-of-a-kind favorites into fabulous quilts with a look all their own. Mix and match blocks, fabrics, and settings to give your quilts your own signature style.

Have fun! You can quilt it!

elements of
a quilt

Once you understand the parts (elements) that make up every quilt, you'll find that making a quilt is a lot easier than you think! No matter how complex the design or how large the finished quilt, the parts of a quilt and the process of assembling it are more or less the same.

A quilt is made up of the quilt top, the batting, and the backing. When you put these three layers together, they become the quilt "sandwich." The edges of the sandwich are bound with fabric so that there are no raw edges. The stitching together of these layers is the technique known as quilting. You can quilt simple or very intricate designs in many different ways.

The Quilt Top

Most quilt tops are made up of rows of blocks. The blocks and rows are sewn together to make the top of the quilt. The simplest block, called a plain block, is just a square of fabric. Many quilt designs are made up of only plain blocks. Other styles of quilts might combine plain blocks and more intricate blocks to form an overall pattern. There are hundreds of traditional and nontraditional block patterns.

To make pieced blocks, sew together two or more fabrics to form units or groups of units. The sewing sequence and the placement of the units create the block pattern.

You can also make blocks that have a fabric or paper foundation. The foundation stabilizes lightweight or slippery fabrics to help you piece the block pattern accurately. After you construct the block, you then remove the paper foundation.

what size is it?

A quilt is like a puzzle. It is very important that you cut and sew accurately so the pieces fit together to form the desired pattern. No matter how many seams you have in the quilt, you must always allow for seam allowances. The seam allowance is the amount of fabric between the line of stitching and the cut edge of the fabric.

The standard seam allowance in quiltmaking is ¼" (6 mm). To allow for the seam allowance, quilt patterns refer to two different sizes: the cut size and the finished size. The cut size is the size of each unit that makes up the block, including the ¼" (6 mm) seam allowance added to *each* side of the unit. The cut size determines the size of the pieces you will cut

from the fabrics. The finished size is the measurement of the unit, from seam to seam, after it is sewn into the quilt top.

Determine the cut size of the units before cutting any fabric. The cut size of the block projects in this book is 12½" (31.5 cm). After you have sewn the block into a quilt top—with ¼" (6 mm) seam allowances—the finished size of the block will be 12" (30.5 cm) square.

Every element of a quilt—from the smallest unit in an intricate block to the quilt binding—relies on the principles of cut size and finished size. Always consider these measurements carefully when making a quilt.

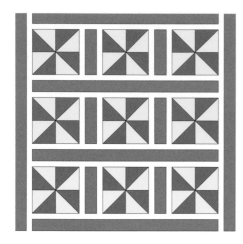

Sashing

When you have made all the blocks you need, you will stitch them together in rows to form the quilt top. Some quilt tops are made with a grid of strips that surround each block. This grid of strips between and around the blocks is known as sashing. Sashing connects the blocks together and also visually separates and highlights each block. Sashing unifies the overall look of the quilt top while also enlarging its size.

Borders

A border is a frame that is added to all four sides of the quilt top. It brings the center of the quilt top into dramatic focus. If the border is the same fabric and width as the sashing, it becomes an extension of the sashing grid, known as the sashing border. Adding one border or more enlarges the size of the quilt top and also adds design interest. Adding borders in different widths creates the effect of a mat and frame enhancing a piece of artwork.

Batting

Batting is the middle layer of the quilt. This layer adds weight, warmth, and thickness to a quilt. Batting is made from cotton, polyester, or wool fibers or from blends of these fibers. It also comes in different thicknesses, which is called loft.

There are many types of batting on the market. In general, low-loft battings are best for machine quilting. High-loft battings are thick and bulky and difficult to guide smoothly through the machine. Batting is sold, precut, and packaged in many sizes, fibers, blends, and lofts. It is sometimes sold by the yard (meter). Refer to the package or ask the sales clerk for information on which is suitable for your project. Buy batting that measures at least 4" (10 cm) wider and longer than the dimensions of the quilt top. The size of batting you'll need for the quilt samplers in this book is indicated in the materials list for each sampler project.

Backing

The backing is the fabric that makes up the back of the quilt. If the quilt top is wider than the backing fabric, you will have to piece the backing to make it the right size. Like the batting, the backing should measure at least 4" (10 cm) wider and longer than the quilt top.

Making the Sandwich

One of the most exciting phases of making a quilt is putting it all together. Suddenly, everything starts to look and feel like a quilt! The first step is to pin together the three layers—quilt top, backing, and batting—to hold them in place while you carry the quilt to the machine and while you stitch.

A quilt sandwich

1. First, prepare the backing. If you need to, piece sections of fabric together so that the backing is the right size for your quilt top. Iron it carefully so that it is wrinkle free. Lay the backing wrong side up on a table or floor—be sure the surface is large enough that you can spread it flat. With masking tape or painter's tape, tape down all the edges so the fabric is smooth and taut.

2. Place the batting over the backing, smoothing it with your hands from the center to the edges.

3. Press the quilt top carefully. Refer to the section Stitching, on page 12, to decide how and where you want to stitch your quilt. If you need to mark the stitching designs on the quilt top, mark them before you add the top to the sandwich. Center the pressed and marked top over the batting and backing. Smooth from the center to the edges.

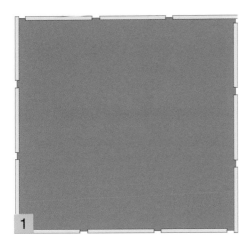

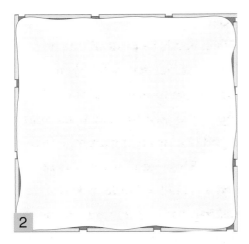

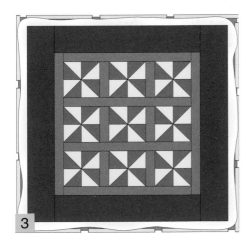

4. Pin the layers of the quilt together securely with quilter's safety pins. Be sure the pins go through all three layers. The pins will keep the layers of the sandwich from shifting when you move the quilt around the sewing machine.

5. Start in the center of the quilt and pin vertically to the top of the quilt. Then, pin vertically from the center to the bottom. Place pins about 4" (10 cm) apart. Do not pin exactly where you will be sewing. For instance, if you will be "stitching in the ditch"—that is, sewing on top of a seam—place pins about 2" (5 cm) or so away from the seam so that you don't have to remove pins while you are stitching.

6. Pin across the width of the quilt, forming a large cross of pins on the quilt top surface. Pin the rest of the quilt top, creating a grid pattern. After you've pinned the entire quilt top, remove the tape. Your sandwich is done, and you are ready to machine-stitch your quilt!

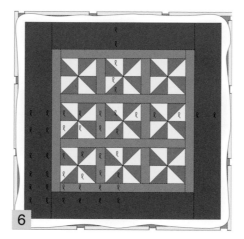

Stitching

You will need to roll up the extra bulk of the quilt to fit it under the arm of the sewing machine. Sit in a chair that is high enough that your wrists are at a right angle to your elbows when your hands are resting on the machine bed. Sit directly in front of the needle of the machine. Start in the center of the area to be quilted and work outward as you

sew. Do not sew over any pins! If a pin is in your stitching path, stop the machine and remove it. Remove the others after you've stitched the entire quilt.

Sew design lines one at a time toward the rolled half of the quilt. The roll will become smaller and smaller as you stitch. When you've reached the edge, turn the quilt and roll the other half to the center, as you did the first. Stitch the rest of the vertical lines in the other direction. Then, roll the quilt horizontally and stitch all the horizontal lines the same way.

Spread your hands and firmly flatten the area you're stitching. Some quilters wear quilting gloves, which will help you keep a firm grip on the fabric. For machine-guided stitching, set the stitch length to sew 8 to 10 stitches per inch (2.5 cm). Guide the quilt through the machine, but do not push or pull the fabric. The even-feed foot will do that for you.

There are two types of machine stitching for quilts: machine-guided stitching and free-motion stitching.

Machine-guided Stitching

With machine-guided stitching, you work with an even-feed, or walking, foot, which feeds the quilt sandwich evenly through the machine as you guide it to make straight or slightly curved lines of stitching. This method is good for stitching in the ditch (page 14), outline stitching, and stitching other straight-line designs.

Start by stitching the vertical lines. Roll half the quilt to the center of the quilt. Put the roll under the machine arm. For a large quilt, accordion-fold the excess quilt in your lap by making small folds in alternating directions.

Free-motion Stitching

Free-motion quilting allows you to sew continuous lines of stitching in various directions across the quilt. You control the stitch length and the design simply by moving the quilt freely under the needle. With a little practice, you will be able to stitch curves and freeform shapes with consistent stitches.

When free-motion stitching, you work with a darning foot or free-motion foot (page 28). You also disengage or "drop" the feed dogs (refer to your sewing machine manual for specific instructions on how to do this on your machine). When you drop the feed dogs, the machine no longer moves the fabric across the bed during stitching. A darning foot, unlike a universal foot, does not hold the fabric in place. Instead, it moves up and down with the needle. By making these machine adjustments, you can easily move the quilt forward, backward, and sideways to control the direction and length of your stitches.

The length of the stitch is controlled by the speed at which you move the quilt and by the speed of the machine. Fast free-motion movements and fast machine speed will produce larger stitches. Slow movements and slow speed will produce smaller stitches. The goal is to make even stitches of consistent length. Put a new, sharp quilting needle in your machine. Set up your machine with the type of foot you need. Wind one or two full bobbins of thread in the color you'll be working with.

here's a hint!

To practice your free-motion quilting skills, make a few "doodle pads"—small quilt sandwiches, at least 12" (30.5 cm) square, made of muslin or scrap fabric.

Stitching in the Ditch: Stitching in the ditch means stitching directly through the center of a stitched seam. The stitching will be almost invisible, but it will emphasize the quilting. Invisible, monofilament thread is great for this type of stitching. Work with cotton thread in the bobbin in a color that matches the back of the quilt. As you sew, do not look at the needle. Instead, look at the seam, about 1" to 2" (2.5 to 5 cm) in front of the needle, to keep you stitching exactly in the "ditch."

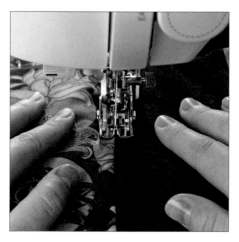

Outline Stitching: Outline stitching is positioned ¼" (6 mm) away from the seam lines to outline the quilt designs. Small quilts are easy to pivot on the sewing machine, so you can outline-stitch with the walking foot. Some walking feet have a

¼" (6 mm) mark to guide you. Sew with the mark positioned on the seam line to keep your stitching an even ¼" (6 mm) away from the seam. Stop ¼" (6 mm) away from a corner with your needle down into the fabric and raise the presser foot. Pivot the quilt, lower the presser foot, and continue sewing. For larger quilts, you'll outline-stitch with a darning foot (page 28) and free-motion quilting (page 12).

Starting and Stopping: To keep your stitching from unraveling, begin and end every line with several very small stitches. For machine-guided stitching, adjust the machine to take very short stitches for about ¼" (6 mm). Then readjust the stitch length to its normal setting. Make the same adjustment as you near the

end of the line of stitching. Next, clip the upper and lower threads, reposition the quilt, and start the next line of quilting. For free-motion stitching, make several tiny stitches at the beginning and the end of your line of stitching by quickly moving the quilt back and forth slightly as you start and stop. This motion will lock your stitches.

Stipple Quilting

Stipple quilting is a very versatile method of free-motion stitching. You can stipple a portion of a block or quilt or the entire surface. Stippling produces an overall pattern—as if you've sewn continuous lines shaped like large pieces of a jigsaw puzzle. Try not to cross over any of the lines of stitching. Your design can be as dense or open as you like.

Be careful not to sew over any pins. Instead, stitch in curves away and around them to create the stippled pattern. Choose a thread that matches the overall color of your quilt top or try a variegated thread to create subtle color changes.

Binding

The binding is the final element of your quilt. It is a narrow strip of continuous fabric that you sew around all the edges of the quilt to enclose the raw edges of the quilt sandwich. The binding adds a thin frame around your finished quilt.

the finishing touch

Your quilt is a work of art! So, it should be signed and dated—just like any other masterpiece. The best way to do this is to add a fabric label to the backing. If there's a story behind the quilt or if you've made it as a gift, put that information on the label, too. You can make your own labels or buy them already made.

"Write" on the label with one or more simple hand-embroidery stitches or with a permanent archival fabric pen. Or, print a photo or saying onto paper-backed fabric to add an extra-special personal touch.

When I'm a grown up woman,
with hair up on my head,
I'll sit and sew
the whole night through,
and never go to bed.

For the
Happy Baby!
Love from Aunt
Katie
2008

Happy Birthday Grandma!
From all of us!

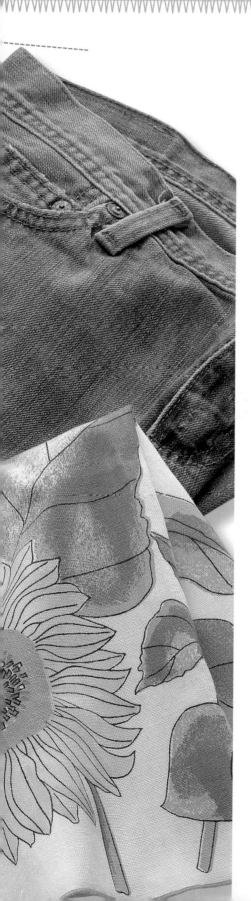

fabrics for quilts

At one time, clothing and fabric were scarce, and quilters hoarded and traded scraps to make their quilts. Modern quilters have the luxury of choosing from the endless selection of beautiful cotton quilting fabrics available in stores, at quilting shows, and online. But your quilt doesn't have to be made only of new fabrics. You can make blocks and block units from small pieces of any type of fabric you like. For example, you might want to repurpose your Aunt Lucy's tablecloth to make a quilt that will always remind you of her. Or you might want to preserve a favorite blouse that doesn't fit anymore or recycle the designs from a great T-shirt. There are lots of ways to get creative in your quilting!

A Few Things about Fabrics

Once you understand these few things about fabric, you'll be able to make good choices about the types of fabrics to choose for your quilts.

Width

The width of the fabric is the measurement from selvage to selvage. A selvage is the finished edge on each side of the fabric. Fabric comes in several widths. Quilter's cotton is 42" to 44" (106.5 to 112 cm) wide. Fashion fabric can be 45" (114.5 cm) or 50" (127 cm) wide.

Length

The length of fabric is the amount that is cut from the bolt or roll of fabric. A yard (36" [91.5 cm]) of fabric that is 44" (112 cm) wide will measure 44" × 36" (112 × 91.5 cm). Fabric cut from a bolt or a roll is called yard goods or yardage.

Right or Wrong?

Sewing instructions always refer to the "right side" and the "wrong side" of the fabric. The right side is the "good" side that is on display in your quilt or block. The wrong side is the reverse side, which will be on the inside of the quilt or block. When you face fabric pieces right sides together and sew seams, the seam allowances are on the inside, or wrong side, of the fabric.

The wrong side of a printed fabric may sometimes look dull or slightly faded. Some fabrics are the same on both sides because of the way they were dyed or printed. If both sides of the fabric look the same, choose either side as the right side for all the quilt pieces so that all the pattern pieces fit together.

Finding Fabrics

Your fabric should be firm and supple enough so you can cut and sew it accurately—but not so heavy that the stitched seams will pull apart. The fabric should also be clean and should iron well. Because there are so many seams in a quilt, the fabric should not be stiff, heavy, or bulky. There should also be minimal raveling at the cut edges.

Cotton

The first choice for quilts is quilter's cotton. It is sturdy, wears well, and is easy to sew and iron. It is widely available by the yard (meter) or in "fat quarters" (see sidebar at right). Quilter's cotton is 42" to 44" (106.5 to 112 cm) wide from selvage to selvage. It's perfect for all the elements of your quilt, from blocks to binding. If you'd like, you can make every block and quilt project in this book entirely of quilter's cotton.

Blocks and block units, which require small pieces, present a good opportunity for combining quilter's cotton with fabric harvested from clothing and other sources. Make the quilt back, sashing, borders, and bindings with quilter's cotton.

who are you calling fat?

Quilters refer to fat quarters when talking about quilter's cotton. What's that all about? A fat quarter is simply a quarter of a yard (meter) of fabric, cut to size specifically for quilting.

A quarter-yard (0.25 m) of fabric cut from the bolt will yield a strip of fabric 9" × 44" (23 × 112 cm). That's a nice, long strip of fabric, but it may not be wide enough for the shapes that a quilter needs. So, quilt shops precut 1 yd. (1 m) of fabric into four pieces that are each 18" × 22" (45.5 × 56 cm). Therefore, a fat quarter is still a quarter-yard (quarter meter) of fabric, but just cut into a different shape.

You can buy one or two fat quarters or a whole bunch. Some coordinated collections of beautiful fabrics are sold together in groups of fat quarters so quilters can quickly add variety to their fabric "stashes."

Other Choices

Clothing and household fabrics are also a good source of quilting fabrics. Garments made from cotton, denim, flannel, silk, and satin are great for repurposing into block units. You can harvest beautiful silks from men's ties, robes, and other garments.

Cotton bandanas, shirts, blouses, and cotton tablecloths and linens (new or vintage) will yield a surprising amount of useful quilting fabric. Just be sure the fabric is about the same weight or a little lighter than quilter's cotton. Fashion fabrics like denim and flannel for clothing are fine, but fabrics made for outerwear or home decoration are too heavy.

Cotton T-shirts and cotton knit fabrics are difficult to cut and sew because they are stretchy and unstable. Fusing interfacing to part of a T-shirt or to knit fabric reduces the stretch, however, and makes it much more suitable for quilting. Fusible interfacings, stabilizers, and webs help hold down the edges of small appliqués. You can stabilize slippery or silky fabrics with a foundation fabric or paper to form crisp and accurate seams.

here's a hint!

No matter how much you love them, don't choose fabrics or garments that are worn out, stained, mildewed, or frayed. Avoid stretch fibers such as spandex, which is difficult to cut and sew, and heavy, stiff, or bulky fabrics, which will not piece well. Skip hand and polyester knits, open weaves, heavy velvets, and home decorating fabrics, too.

Cleaning Fabrics

When choosing fabrics, always think about how you will use the finished quilt. Decorative quilts—used as wall hangings or table toppers—won't get a lot of wear and probably won't need to be laundered. So, feel free to select silky fabrics, satins, and vintage linens.

A functional quilt—a bed quilt or a throw for the couch—will get more wear, so it needs to be washable. Make sure all the fabrics in the quilt are washable. Quilts should not be washed too frequently, however, so always treat them with care.

Washing Washable Fabrics

If you are working with washable fabrics, be sure to wash, dry, and iron all the different fabrics in the quilt before you cut and sew them.

You can wash and dry cotton and other washable fabrics by machine (but check the care labels on any articles of clothing). Sort items by color and wash on the gentle cycle. Do not use fabric softeners because they make it difficult to work with fusibles and stabilizers. Tumble-dry on low heat and remove the fabrics while they are still damp. Iron out the wrinkles and refold the

fabric. Keep chlorine bleach away from old printed cottons or linens. If you are not sure whether a garment or fabric is washable, test it. Cut a small square from the garment or fabric and wash and dry it with a small piece of white cotton. If the square shrinks or changes texture more than you like—or if the color has bled onto the white cotton—consider dry-cleaning the fabric and save it for a decorative quilt you won't need to wash.

here's a hint!

After buying or gathering fabric, sort your treasures. Toss them into baskets or boxes marked "Wash Me!" "Test Me!" "Clean Me!" Leave them in the laundry room or near the hamper. Wash them as you have time and then put them away.

Washing Silks and Satins

Before you cut silk or satin garments and accessories—for example, women's scarves and men's ties—you should either dry-clean them or wash them in cold water and a mild detergent (by hand or machine). You could also wash them in a good-quality shampoo that doesn't con-

tain creme rinse (silk is a natural fiber made of protein, like human hair). Satins can be made of a variety of different fibers from silk to polyester. Test a small piece before washing the whole piece or garment.

Cutting Fabrics

Accurate cutting is very important to ensure that all the elements of the quilt fit together. Quilters use rotary tools for fast and efficient cutting (see page 30). Gather your tools and read these instructions before starting. (The directions are written for a right-handed person. If you are left-handed, change the blade in your cutter to the other side and reverse these directions to accommodate.) Practice cutting on a large piece of scrap fabric until you feel comfortable with the tools and your cutting is accurate.

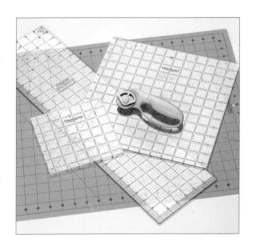

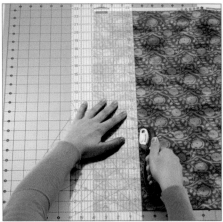

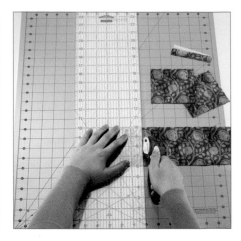

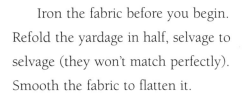

The first cut produces a clean, straight edge, which will guide you in making the next cuts accurately.

Working with the ruler or the mat grid-lines as a guide, cut the strip to the width you need.

Measuring from a clean-cut edge, cut the strip into squares or rectangles of the dimension you need.

Iron the fabric before you begin. Refold the yardage in half, selvage to selvage (they won't match perfectly). Smooth the fabric to flatten it.

When cutting fabric yardage, cut strips to the desired width. Then, cut across the strips to get the size units you need. For example, if you need four 4½" (11.5 cm) squares and two 4½" × 6½ " (11.5 × 16.5 cm) rectangles, cut a strip that is 4½" (11.5 cm) wide. Then, crosscut the strips into squares and rectangles of the correct size.

Always align the edge of the fabric with the grid markings on the cutting mat to cut a straight edge. Double-check the sizes you need and slide the ruler over the fabric until you reach the right measurement. Align the ruler with the grid markings and cut.

Making the First Cut

The first cut will create a clean, straight edge. You'll measure all the following cuts from this new edge. If you are working with yardage, lay the folded fabric on the cutting mat with the bulk of it to the left and the folded edge at the bottom.

If you are working with a fat quarter or an irregularly shaped scrap of fabric, open the fabric and iron it. Lay the fabric flat on the mat. Lay the ruler on the fabric to the left of the raw edges. Align a horizontal line of the ruler with the bottom of the fabric. Align the vertical edge of the ruler with the vertical gridline on the mat—above and below the horizontal fabric edges.

Stand while you cut. Spread your left hand open on the ruler, well away from the ruler's edge and the path of the blade. Apply pressure so the ruler won't shift. Position the rotary cutter against the edge of the ruler. Apply pressure as you roll the cutter against the edge of the ruler and away from you. Roll along the entire length of the fabric. Always roll the blade away from you.

If you need to cut only one piece, work with the square ruler.

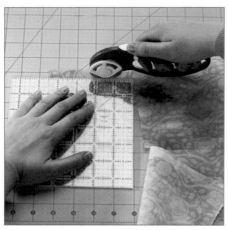

Realign the edges of the fabric and ruler to continue cutting the square.

Cutting Strips

Carefully turn the fabric so the newly cut edge is on your left and the bulk of the fabric is on your right. If you are working with folded fabric, try to avoid disturbing the newly cut edge. Align the fabric edge with the gridlines of the mat. Double-check the dimensions of the pieces you need. Position the ruler and cut the first strip to the desired width. If your ruler is not wide enough, use the markings on the mat.

Crosscutting

Unfold the strip and position it so that the bulk of it is to the left of the ruler. Align the long, bottom edge of the strip with a horizontal line on your ruler. Make a narrow cut to clean-cut and square the edge.

Turn the strip so that the squared-up edge is on the left and the bulk of the strip is on the right. Align the bottom of the strip with a horizontal gridline on the mat. Measure and cut the width you need to make the finished shape.

Cutting Squares

Sometimes you need to cut only one piece to make a plain block. The easiest way to do this is with a square ruler—just be sure the ruler is larger than the fabric square you want.

Position the square ruler in a corner of the fabric. Allow an extra ½" (1.3 cm) or so to extend on the bottom and the right edge of the ruler. Hold the ruler down firmly with your left hand, keeping your hand away from the right and top edges of the ruler. Cut up the right side of the ruler and across the top.

Next, turn the fabric around and align the cut edges with the markings on the ruler that correspond with the size you are cutting. Cut the remaining sides.

Harvesting Fabric from Garments

After you have selected the garments or other items you'd like to repurpose in your quilt, be sure to wash the entire item and allow it to dry thoroughly. To harvest pieces for your quilt, first remove any seams by cutting them out with scissors. Remove zippers, buttons, and labels, too. Rough-cut the fabric to shape. After you iron the fabric, you'll cut more precise pieces with rotary tools to the sizes you need for the block units. Leave a little fabric around any garment details that you'd like to use in your quilt as well.

tools and notions

The sewing machine is the quilter's ultimate tool—from start to finish. The only stitch you need for patchwork piecing, foundation piecing, and assembling the quilt top is a straight stitch. For appliqué, you'll need some of the decorative stitches found on most machines. After the layers are sandwiched together, you'll stitch it together and bind it on the sewing machine.

Quilters collect tools and fabrics so they are ready to go whenever they get the "quilting bug." The essential tools you'll need—plus a few other basic tools—are presented in this chapter. Keep everything tucked neatly in a box or basket, especially small, sharp items. Store tools close to your fabric stash. That way, you'll have everything you need when the quilting bug hits!

Know Your Machine

Once you understand the workings of your machine, almost any kind of sewing is possible. You should be comfortable threading the machine, winding bobbins, adjusting the stitch length and width, changing presser feet, and lowering the "feed dogs." Get to know your machine with the help of the instructional manual, CD, or DVD the manufacturer provided.

Machine Parts

Sewing machines may look slightly different from each other, but they all work much the same way. Here are the basic parts you'll want to know about.

Hand Wheel: The hand wheel raises and lowers the needle while the machine is sewing. Turning the hand wheel toward you when the machine is stopped will allow you to raise and lower the needle—helpful when removing fabric, repositioning fabric under the needle, pivoting at corners, and sewing around curves.

Some machines have a "needle down" feature, which automatically stops the machine with the needle in its lowest position. Activate this feature while appliquéing.

Stitch Length Control: This control adjusts the length of the stitch. For general sewing, 10 to 12 stitches per inch (2.5 cm) is fine. For piecing blocks and sewing the quilt top and the backing, work with a slightly shorter stitch length. When stitching your quilt sandwich, use a longer stitch length.

Stitch Width Control: This control adjusts the width of zigzag and other decorative stitches. (Straight stitches do not have width.) Not all feet can accommodate every stitch width. Be sure to select the correct presser foot for the type of stitch you are sewing. Check your machine manual.

Presser Foot: The presser foot holds the fabric in place while you sew. Raise the presser foot to position the fabric. Lower the presser foot to sew.

Different types of sewing require different presser feet, which are easy to attach and remove. Most machines come with a basic set of presser feet, which includes a universal (or all-purpose) presser foot, a zipper foot, and a buttonhole foot. You can purchase additional styles, but check your manual first to be sure they are compatible with your model of machine.

Feed Dogs: The feed dogs are the ridged teeth in the stitch plate, below the presser foot. The presser foot keeps the fabric in contact with the feed dogs. Together, the presser foot and feed dogs move the fabric smoothly through the machine while the needle forms stitches.

For free-motion quilting, you must drop or disengage the feed dogs so you can move the fabric freely as you stitch.

Stitch Plate: The stitch plate has an opening for the needle to pass through. On some machines, the stitch plate has etched lines that provide stitching guides for accurate, consistent seam allowances.

Quilting Table

Some machines come with an extension table that slides onto the machine. The table provides a larger surface to work on. It makes piecing and appliqué a snap because more of your block lies flat as you sew, and the large pieces of fabric slide easily as you maneuver your quilt under the needle. Extension tables are often a standard accessory, or you can purchase one to fit your specific machine.

Quilting Feet

Here are four specific presser feet you'll need for quilting. The exact styles may vary with different models of sewing machines, but their function remains the same. Some of these feet may come with your machine. If not, you can purchase them separately. Always store extra presser feet with your machine.

Quarter-inch Foot

Although it's not essential, the quarter-inch foot is the most useful foot for piecing the elements of a quilt. In quilting, the standard seam allowance is ¼" (6 mm). The edge of this foot falls exactly ¼" (6 mm) away from the needle. By using the edge of the foot as a guide, you'll have an accurate ¼" (6 mm) seam every time. Some styles even have markings to make it easier to turn a corner at exactly ¼" (6 mm). Some quarter-inch feet even have an attached guide that helps hold the layers of fabric directly under the foot.

Open-toe or Satin Foot

There are many versions of the open-toe embroidery foot (sometimes called a satin foot). They all have a cut-away opening or a clear plastic section at the front. Some are made entirely of clear plastic so you can see precisely where you are

here's a hint!

To make your own stitching guide, measure ¼" (6 mm) to the right of the needle. If there isn't already a line at that spot on the stitch plate or bobbin cover, make one by sticking a short stack of sticky notes right on the line. As you sew, line up the raw edge of the fabric against the paper's edge for an accurate seam allowance. When the top sticky note gets dog-eared and curls, just pull it off the stack and keep sewing!

sewing—wonderful for appliqué, satin stitching, and other decorative stitching. Usually there is a groove or "tunnel" on the underside of the foot, which allows dense stitching to pass freely, without jamming.

Even-Feed Foot

Whenever you're sewing together multiple layers of fabric, you'll work with the even-feed, or walking, foot. This foot does the same work as the feed dogs, but on the top surface of the fabric. The even-feed foot moves the top layers of the quilt sandwich through the machine at the same rate as the bottom layers, which are being moved by the machine's feed dogs. Without an even-feed foot, the layers of the sandwich will feed through the machine unevenly, causing puckers, wrinkles, and skipped stitches on the quilt back. You can also use the even-feed foot to sew on the binding.

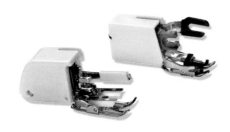

Darning/Embroidery Foot

The darning/embroidery foot is the foot you use to free-motion-stitch the quilt sandwich. The foot moves up and down as the needle stitches, and it has a circular or square "hoop" that holds the fabric flat and keeps it

moving smoothly as you stitch. Some styles have a spring to hold the fabric securely in place. Other types have an opening in the hoop or are made of clear plastic to make it easy to see where you're stitching.

Quilter's Tool Kit

There are tools for every kind of sewing—including special tools for quilting. Here's an assortment of essential quilting tools you'll want to have handy, as well as a few simple sewing tools.

Machine Needles

Machine needles dull with use, so they should be changed frequently. A good rule of thumb is to change the needle after a total of six to ten hours of sewing. It might be easier to remember to change it whenever you start a new quilt top or when you start to stitch your sandwich together. Never sew over pins,

because they might nick, bend, or even break the needle.

Machine needles come in a range of sizes and types for different sewing tasks and threads. Make a habit of keeping an assortment on hand. Some brands color-code needle types so you can see at a glance which one you're using. Needle sizes usually are marked in both metric and standard measurements. Metric sizes appear first. The lower the number, the finer the needle is.

here's a hint!

When you put a new needle in your machine, tape the small needle package to the side or top of your machine—or anywhere it won't interfere with threading or sewing. With just a glance, you can always check which size and type needle you are using.

The following is a list of sizes and types of needles for quiltmaking, their uses, and their compatibility with different threads.

Universal or sharp/microtex needles: These general-purpose needles are great for piecing together the elements of the quilt top. Sizes 70/11 to 80/12 work well with 100 percent cotton and cotton/poly threads and with invisible nylon thread.

Quilting needles: These needles will smoothly pierce several layers of fabrics. Choose a 75/11 for machine-stitching your quilt sandwich and adding binding. If you use a 100 percent cotton thread marked for machine quilting—which is slightly thicker than regular thread— switch to a 90/14 size quilting needle.

Embroidery needles: These needles are for decorative, dense stitching, such as the satin stitch. A 75/11 needle is suitable for machine embroidery and stitching with rayon threads.

Threads

There is a wide variety of threads available for all aspects of quiltmaking—in a rainbow of colors. There are even variegated threads that change from one color to another as you sew. General-purpose cotton and cotton/polyester threads are strong and well suited to cotton quilting fabrics. Good-quality, 100 percent cotton thread or a cotton/polyester blend thread are good for piecing and general sewing. Also consider using machine-quilting cotton thread (never use hand-quilting threads in the sewing machine).

For stitching in the ditch, many quilters like to use invisible nylon thread. The stitching adds definition to the quilt pattern but doesn't show. Invisible thread comes in clear and a "smoke" shade, which is good on dark fabrics.

For visible and decorative stitching, you have many thread choices. Rayon and machine embroidery threads have added sheen and are beautiful with decorative stitching. The more you quilt, the more you will want to experiment with thread types, but you can simply start with the basics. Just wind your bobbin with 100 percent cotton thread, matching the thread color to the color of the quilt backing. Use the same thread—in the same or a different color—in the needle.

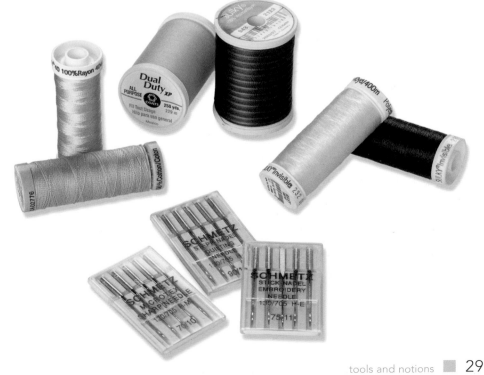

what color thread?

There are so many colors in a quilt, how do you decide which color thread you should choose for piecing?

Most quilters choose neutral colors—white, light gray, or tan for light-colored or pastel fabrics and medium gray for medium- and dark-colored fabrics. Wind the bobbin with the same color thread that you use in the needle. A neutral shade of thread won't clash with other colors and sometimes won't show at all, so you won't need to change thread each time you start stitching a new quilt fabric. If you need to rip out a line of stitching, the stitches will be easy to find, too.

Rotary Cutting Tools

The fastest and most accurate way to cut fabric for quiltmaking is with rotary cutting—a technique that requires a rotary cutter, an acrylic ruler, and a cutting mat (see page 21). These three tools, which are always used together, are sold separately and in sets.

Rotary cutters come in three different sizes: 28 mm, 45 mm, and 60 mm. The 45 mm size is the most versatile for quilting. There are many styles and brands but all have either a retractable cover or blade lock so that the sharp cutting edge is safely concealed when the tool is not in use. Make it a habit to close the cover or lock the blade every time you put down the cutter—and put the tool away when you're through working! Rotary cutter blades will get dull with use, so buy extra blades and carefully change blades according to the manufacturer's directions on the package.

As you're cutting, the cushioned cutting mat protects your work surface from damage. These durable mats are printed with a grid of inches and/or centimeters to help you cut with accuracy. A mat that is at least 18" × 24" (45.5 × 61 cm) is a versatile size.

Clear acrylic rulers for rotary cutting are sold in many shapes and sizes. They also have grids and measurements printed on them to help you cut accurately. Rulers should have markings in ⅛" to 1" (3 mm to 2.5 cm) increments. A 6½" × 24" (16.5 × 61 cm) ruler is a good size for cutting yardage, fabric strips, and geometrically shaped pieces.

Although they're not essential, square rulers, which come in a variety of sizes, are extremely useful. The cut size of all the block projects in this book is 12½" (31.5 cm), so you'll find a ruler that is at least 12½" (31.5 cm) square very handy. This tool makes it a snap to trim and "square" your blocks and the corners of the quilt top. A 6½" (16.5 cm) square ruler is a good size for smaller squares and shapes. Collect rulers of other shapes and sizes as you find you need them.

Measuring and Marking

A flexible tape measure is a big help when measuring yardage, sashing and border strips, and other large pieces of fabric. Fiberglass or plastic tape measures come in two sizes: 60" (152.5 cm) and 120" (305 cm), both useful to have when working with large quilts.

There are fabric "pencils" of all kinds and colors that are made for marking quilts. Always test them first on a scrap of your fabric to be sure they do not leave a permanent mark. Easy-to-use chalk dispensing tools leave a precise line that brushes off easily. Permanent, archival marking pens are great for making labels and signing your quilts. They come in many colors and styles. Be sure to choose those that are suitable for fabric and are washable.

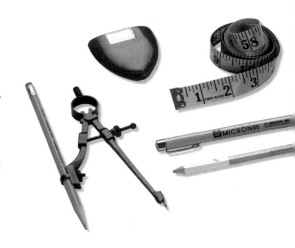

making a design wall

A design wall lets you play with unit combinations as you're designing your blocks to find which you like best. You can sample fabric and color choices or lay out your entire quilt top to preview the overall pattern before you begin to sew. It's a great tool!

To make a design wall, tape or tack white cotton flannel—or a flannel-backed tablecloth—to a wall. You could also hang or clip the flannel over a door. The cotton quilting fabric will stick to the flannel without pins, so you can move the units and blocks around easily until you find a combination that works for you. Some flannel is made with a printed grid, which is perfect for designing blocks.

You can also simply cover a large piece of foam core board. Secure the flannel on the back of the board with masking tape. This smaller design wall is lightweight, and you can prop it up on a chair or against the wall when you're working and easily store it behind a door when you're not.

Ironing and Pressing Tools

Ironing is essential. You can cut and sew any fabric more easily and more accurately after it has been ironed. The process of sliding the warm iron back and forth on the fabric smoothes out wrinkles and prepares the fabric so you can begin to work with it.

Pressing is a different technique. When you press a fabric, you apply heat by putting the iron down firmly on the surface and then lifting it off. As you sew the pieces of your quilt, it's important to press them as you go. Pressing ensures flat seams and sharp edges.

In quilting, the seam allowances are usually pressed to one side, to reduce bulk. Always follow the project instructions for the correct way to press the seams. Pressing correctly will help the quiltmaking process.

When pressing delicate fabrics or working with fusibles, work with a press cloth to protect the fabric and the iron. Some fusibles require a damp press cloth, so check the product information. When working with printed T-shirts, press with a damp press cloth between the shirt and the iron so that neither is damaged by smearing or melting ink from the printed design.

You can buy a press cloth or make one from lightweight, white or light-colored cotton fabric. A 14" (35.5 cm) square is a good size.

Rippers and Nippers

A seam ripper is an essential tool for any kind of sewing. At some point, every sewer stitches a crooked seam or puts two pieces of fabric together the wrong way. The only thing to do in those cases is to rip out the seam and sew it again. That's where the seam ripper comes in.

Every few stitches, you simply slip the seam ripper's tiny blade under a stitch and cut it. Then you flip to the other side of the seam and lift the thread with the tip of the ripper. Repeat the process to pull out the entire line of stitches. Clean up any remaining little bits of cut thread with a lint roller or a piece of tape.

Because there are so many seams in quiltmaking, a thread nipper is also a great tool to have. Keep the nipper by the machine so you can easily clip threads as you work. This way, the thread ends won't slip between seams as you continue to sew pieces together. It's much easier to clip them as you go than to remove them later. Small, sharp scissors will also do the job.

Pins

Straight quilting pins are long and thin and slide smoothly through layers of fabric. They're great for holding pieces together while you're sewing. Flat-head or flower pins lie flat on your fabric and are easy to

see. They're perfect as temporary fabric markers. You can write numbers directly on the flat heads with a fine-point marker. These pins won't get in your way or fall out.

Safety pins will keep the three layers of the quilt sandwich together as you stitch. Nonrusting safety pins in size 1 or 2 are best. Curved pins are even easier to get through all the layers. No need to close the pins when you put them away—just store them in a box or jar with the points open, and they're ready to use when you need them.

Where there are pins, there must be a pincushion or two! Keep a small one on or near the machine as you sew and another one on your work surface.

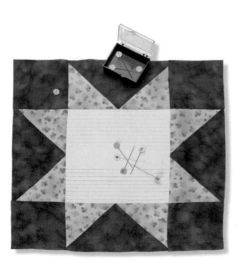

before you sew

After you've picked your project and prepared your materials, you're ready to start to sew. Set up your machine, wind a couple of bobbins with neutral-colored thread, and gather together your tools.

Position the iron and ironing board near the machine. Keep your seam ripper and thread nipper (or small scissors) close at hand and stored in a small basket, box, or tray to prevent them from falling to the floor. Also keep your pincushion nearby.

As you pin, position the pinheads to the right of the raw edge of the fabric and perpendicular to the line of stitching. This way, as you sew, it will be easy to pull the pins out of the fabric before they reach the needle. Never sew over a pin. Just slow down or stop stitching completely as you come to it, remove it, and put it right into the pincushion.

Your job as you sew is to guide the fabric through the machine, maintaining a consistent ¼" (6 mm) seam allowance. The feed dogs will move the fabric along the machine bed without your having to push or pull the fabric. Keep your eyes on the fabric in front of the needle and you'll have better control of the stitching line. Remember, you don't need to backstitch when piecing because every row of stitching will be intersected by another seam.

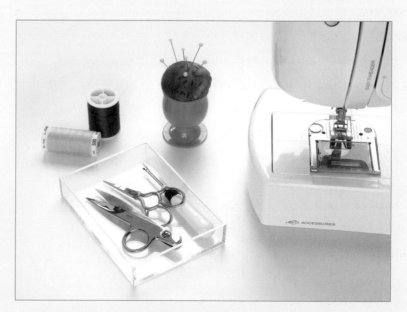

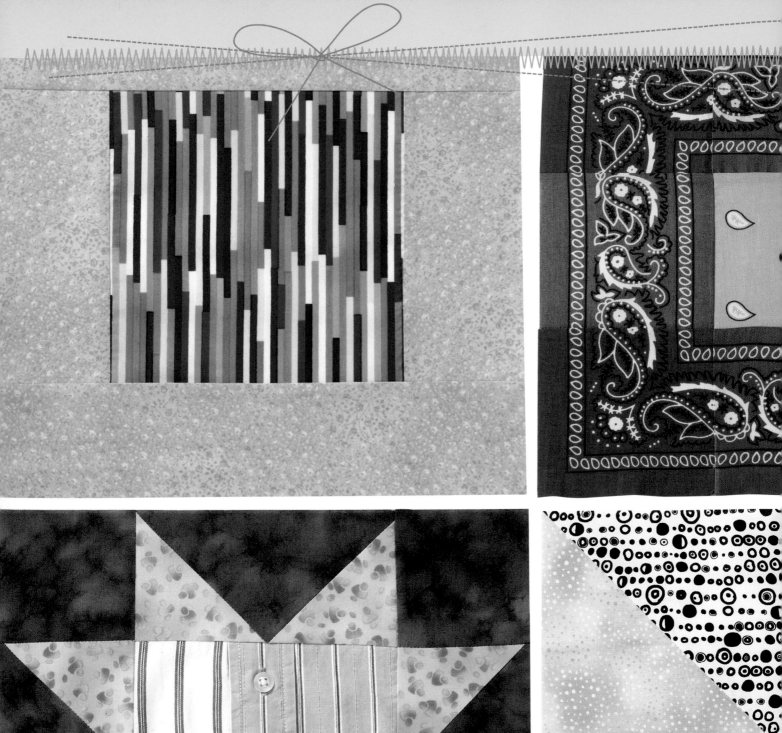
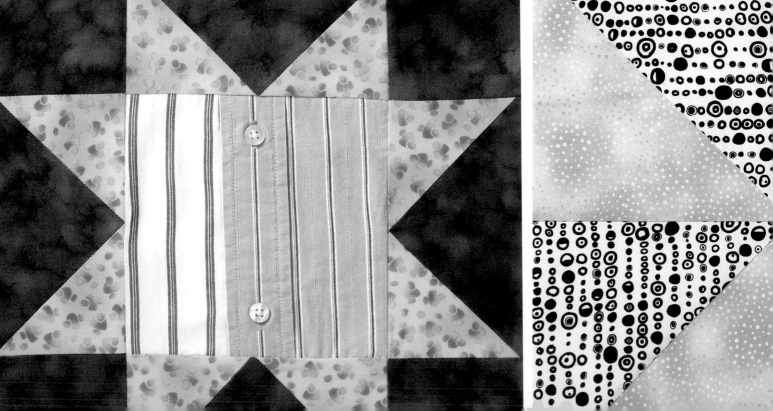

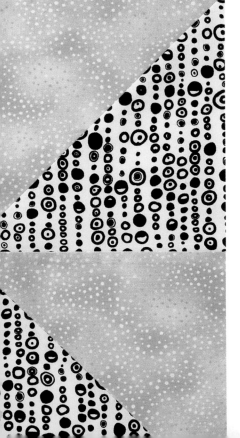

patchwork piecing

Piecing—the simple process of sewing together pieces of fabric—is the basis of all quiltmaking, from making the blocks to adding the binding. By making the four blocks in this chapter—including the Bandana Fofanna Nine-Patch Block (made with your drawerful of colorful bandanas) to the Button-Down Sawtooth Star Block (made with repurposed shirts), you will soon master the basic skills that you will apply every time you make a quilt.

The last project in this chapter, the Dress Casual Quilt, is a sampler of all the techniques you've learned and a great first quilt. Everything you need to know to finish the quilt is in the project. So, let's start sewing!

five easy pieces block

This first block is made up of five fabric units and four seams. Simple, right? But don't let the simplicity fool you—the design is quite versatile. Choose two exciting fabrics to make it bright and fun. It's also a good block to show off a special fabric you'd like to feature, as if it were a picture in a frame. By making this block, you'll learn the basic principles of piecing and making borders.

Project Facts

- **Cut Size:** 12½" (31.5 cm) square
- **Finished Size:** 12" (30.5 cm) square

Find Your Fabrics

- Two cotton fabrics, ¼ yd. (0.25 m) of each or one fat quarter of each

Note: All fabric amounts are based on 42" to 44" (106.5 to 112 cm)-wide quilter's cotton.

Cutting List

- **From Fabric A:**
  Cut one 7½" (19 cm) square.
- **From Fabric B:**
  Cut two 3" × 7½" (7.5 × 19 cm) strips and two 3" × 12½" (7.5 × 31.8 cm) strips.

five easy pieces block

1 Cut your fabrics, referring to the cutting list on page 37. With right sides together, pin the shorter strips to the opposite sides of the square. Sew each seam.

2 Press the seams toward the strips.

3 Pin the longer strips to the top and bottom of the square. Sew the seams and press the new seams toward the strips. The finished Five Easy Pieces Block should measure 12½" (31.5 cm) square.

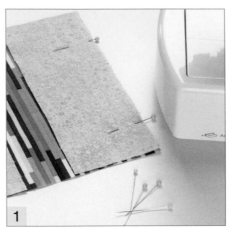

That's all
there is to it!

perfect piecing

In quilt making, accuracy in cutting and sewing is essential. Otherwise, the block units and quilt elements will not fit together. Remember, the seam allowance should be ¼" (6 mm).

Sometimes, the combination of cutting and sewing yields a unit that is slightly shorter or longer than it should be. As long as the difference is slight— ¹⁄₁₆" to ⅛" (2 to 3 mm)—it can be fixed. To make the pieces fit, stretch them slightly or ease extra fullness across the length of the seam. If the size of the pieces is off by more than ⅛" (3 mm), you need to recut them. Too much stretching, for example, will cause the pieces to ripple and pucker.

Here are the simple steps to fit two slightly different-size pieces together.

1. Cut your fabrics, referring to the cutting list on page 37. Then fold each unit in half to find its center.

2. Press the units lightly. Mark each center with a pin.

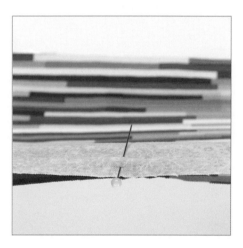

3. Arrange the pieces, positioning the longer piece on the bottom. With right sides together, pin the pieces together at the centers and at the ends.

Sew the pieces together, gently pulling the lower fabric between the pins to ease it evenly across the piece.

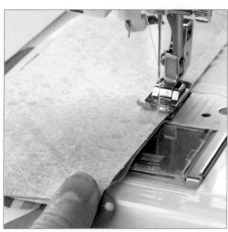

bandana fofanna nine-patch block

This colorful block will add sassy style to any quilt! The Bandana Fofanna Nine-Patch Block is made from three bright bandanas—which can be old favorites or brand new. If you'd like, you can make this block from other types of fabrics instead. As its name suggests, the nine-patch block is made with nine units. Simple piecing and careful pressing will make your seams match perfectly.

Project Facts

- **Cut Size:** 12½" (31.5 cm) square
- **Finished Size:** 12" (30.5 cm) square

Find Your Fabrics

- Three cotton bandanas or three fabrics ¼ yd. (0.25 m) each or three fat quarters quilter's cotton (A, B, C)

Note: All fabric amounts are based on 42" to 44" (106.5 to 112 cm)-wide quilter's cotton.

Cutting List

- **From Bandana/Fabric A:**
  Cut one 4½" (11.5 cm) square.
- **From Bandana/Fabric B:**
  Cut four 4½" (11.5 cm) squares.
- **From Bandana/Fabric C:**
  Cut four 4½" (11.5 cm) squares.

bandana fofanna nine-patch block

1   Cut your squares, following the cutting list on page 41. If you are working with bandanas as your fabric, cut off the narrow rolled hems before you cut your squares.

2   Decide on the nine-patch layout you'd like to have. Lay the pieces on your board or work surface.

3   With right sides together, pin together two squares and then sew them with a ¼" (6 mm) seam allowance.

4   Pin and sew a third square to form the first row.

5   Continue pinning and sewing squares in this way to make all three rows.

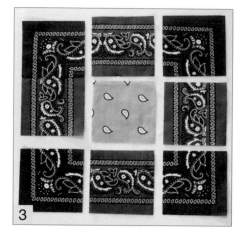

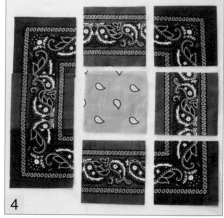

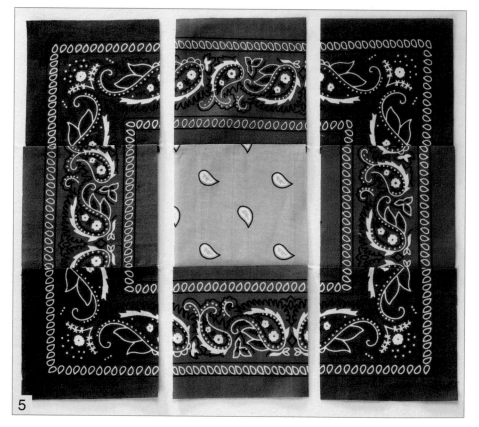

6 Press all the seams of the two outer rows in one direction. Press the seams of the middle row in the opposite direction.

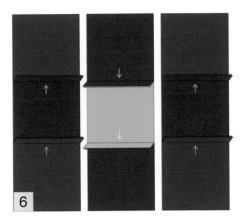

7 With right sides together, pin together rows one and two at the intersection of the seams, carefully matching the seam lines. The seams should butterfly in opposite directions and lie flat. Add pins between the seams if needed. If the ends of the rows don't match exactly, that's okay—it's more important to have the seams line up.

8 Sew, removing the pin at the seam inter-section as you near it and using your finger to hold down the fabric until it passes under the needle to keep the seams from shifting. Press the seam to one side.

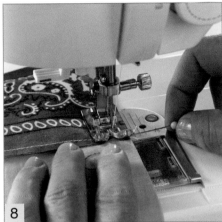

9 Pin row three to row two, matching the seams. Sew and press the seam to one side.

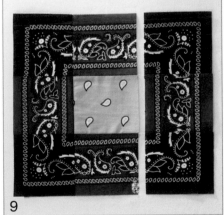

matching seams

By pressing the seam allowances of each row in opposite directions, the seams will "butterfly" and lie flat against one another. This butterfly effect reduces bulk and makes it possible to perfectly match your seams. For a block with only three rows, it doesn't matter which direction you press the seams, as long as the seams of the middle row are pressed in the direction opposite from the seams in the two outer rows.

What a cute way to start a quilt!

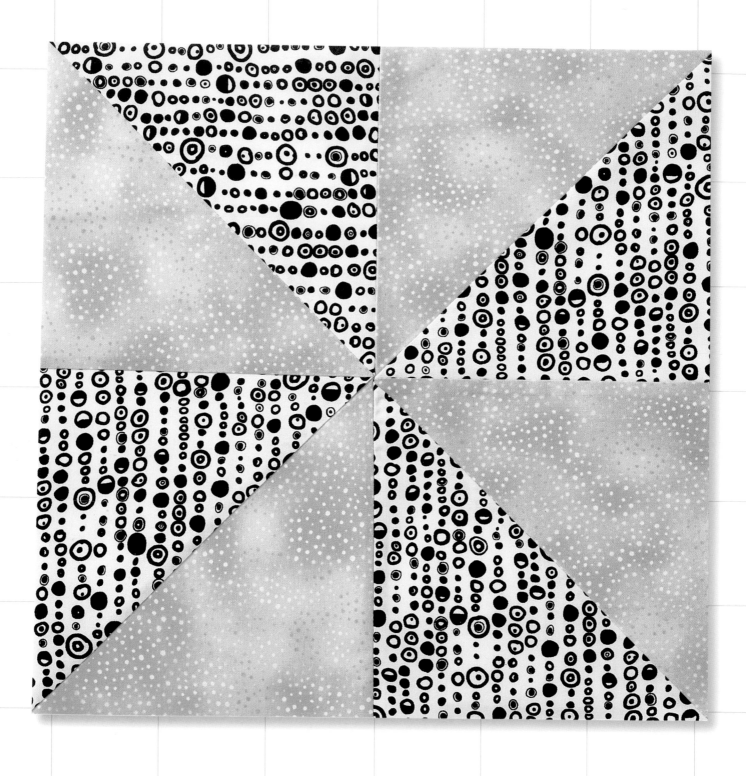

night-and-day pinwheel block

A pinwheel block is made up of four half-triangle squares. With a few quick triangle tricks, this block practically makes itself. The quilt on page 8 contains only this one block, repeated with different fabrics. The Night-and-Day Pinwheel Block also appears in the Dress Casual Quilt on page 52. Compare these two quilts to see how the same block can create very different effects.

Project Facts

- **Cut Size:** 12½" (31.5 cm) square
- **Finished Size:** 12" (30.5 cm) square

Find Your Fabrics

- Two cotton fabrics, ¼ yd. (0.25 m) of each or one fat quarter of each fabric

Note: All fabric amounts are based on 42" to 44" (106.5 to 112 cm)-wide quilter's cotton.

Cutting List

- **From Fabric A and Fabric B:**
  Cut two 6⅞" (17.2 cm) squares.

Notions

- chalk marker or fabric pencil
- ruler with ⅛" (3 mm) markings

night-and-day pinwheel block

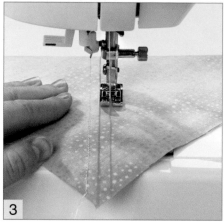

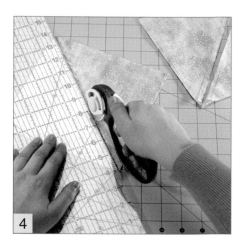

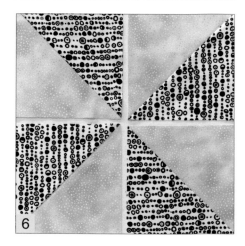

1 Cut the fabric squares, following the cutting list on page 45. On the wrong side of the lighter fabric squares (fabric A), draw a line diagonally down their centers, working with a chalk marker or fabric pencil and a ruler. On each of these squares, draw a second line ¼" (6 mm) from the centerline on one side.

Turn the square in the opposite direction. Draw a third line ¼" (6 mm) from the centerline. The two outer lines are sewing lines. The middle line is the cut line—but don't cut yet. (If you have a ¼" [6 mm] foot for your machine, you do not need to mark the outer lines. The edge of the foot will guide you.)

2 With right sides together, lay a marked square on top of an unmarked fabric square (fabric B). Pin across the marked centerline with two or three pins. Repeat with the remaining marked and unmarked squares.

3 Stitch along one of the outer lines. (If you are using a ¼" [6 mm] foot, line up the edge of the foot with the centerline and sew.) Stitch off the end of the square, turn the square in the other direction, and stitch along the second outer line. Repeat with both sets of squares.

4 Cut the centerline of each square, between the rows of stitching.

5 Press the seams toward one of the fabrics. Clip off the triangle points with small scissors.

6 Arrange the four squares in the pinwheel design on your table or design board.

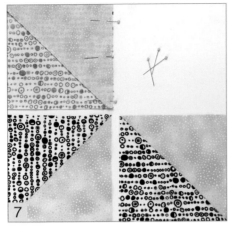

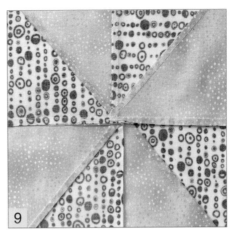

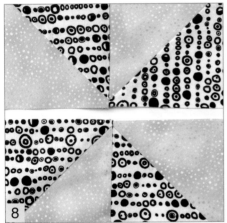

half-square triangle units

The squares for the Night-and-Day Pinwheel Block are cut to 6⅞" (17.2 cm). How do these squares make a 12" (30.5 cm) finished size block? The answer lies in the half-square triangle units.

When working with triangles, the diagonal seam allowance takes up an extra amount of fabric. To allow for this take-up, you need to add an additional ⅞" (2.2 cm) to the cut size of the squares that form the triangles. In other words, the cut size is ⅞" (2.2 cm) larger than the finished size of the square unit.

When you stitch together four half-square triangle units, the block will be 12½" (31.5 cm) square—the cut size of the block. After you have sewn the block into the quilt, it will measure 12" (30.5 cm) square—the finished size of the block.

7 Pin one square on top of the other, with the right sides together. Do the same with the second set of squares. Sew. Press the seams in the opposite directions.

8 It may appear that something is wrong with the way the triangles are sewn into the units. Don't panic! Remember, the seam allowance has not yet been taken up by the seam. When you sew the next seam, the points of the triangle should line up perfectly.

9 With right sides together, pin the remaining seam. Start pinning at the intersection of seams. Then pin toward the outside edges. The seams should butterfly (see page 43). Sew, stitching carefully across the intersection of the diagonal and straight seams. You will have a perfect triangle point.

10 Press open the last seam.

Contrasting fabrics give this
simple block lots of style.

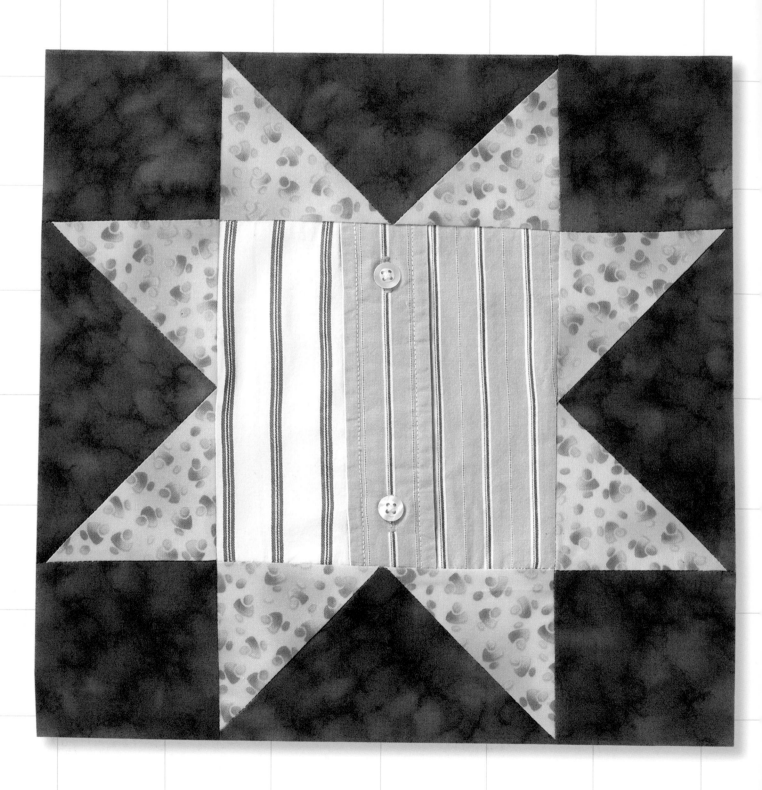

button-down sawtooth star block

The sawtooth star pattern is a variation of the nine-patch block. Instead of having nine units that are all the same size, this block has a very large middle square as the center of the star. Four small corner squares and four double, half-square triangle units make up the rest of the "patches."

You can make this block with all-cotton fabrics, but for fun, this one has a center unit made from two recycled men's shirts that are buttoned together! "Harvest" a favorite old shirt or blouse and give it a try!

Project Facts
- **Cut Size:** 12½" (31.5 cm) square
- **Finished Size:** 12" (30.5 cm) square

Find Your Fabrics
- **Fabric A:** one fat quarter or ¼ yd. (0.25 m) of cotton fabric or a harvested fabric at least 8" (20.5 cm) square
- **Fabric B:** one fat quarter or ¼ yd. (0.25 m) of cotton fabric
- **Fabric C:** one fat quarter or ¼ yd. (0.25 m) of cotton fabric

Note: All fabric amounts are based on 42" to 44" (106.5 to 112 cm)-wide quilter's cotton.

Cutting List
- **From Fabric A:**
  Cut one 6½" (16.5 cm) square.
- **From Fabric B (purple in photo):**
  Cut four 3½" × 6½" (9 × 16.5 cm) rectangles plus four 3½" (9 cm) squares.
- **From Fabric C (yellow in photo):**
  Cut eight 3½" (9 cm) squares.

Notions
- chalk marker or fabric pencil

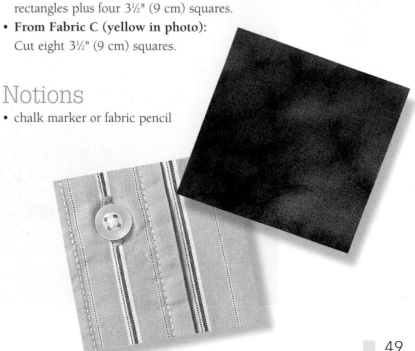

button-down sawtooth star block

1 Cut the fabrics, following the cutting list on page 49. To harvest a garment for the center square (fabric A), follow the instructions in the top sidebar on the facing page.

2 Next, make four double half-square triangle units. You'll mark and assemble these units in a slightly different way than you did the triangles in the Night-and-Day Pinwheel Block on page 44.

3 With a chalk marker or fabric pencil, draw a diagonal line on the wrong side of the eight fabric C squares. The marked line will be the sewing line. With right sides together, pin one marked square to one corner of each fabric B rectangle. (You will have four fabric B squares left over.)

4 Sew along each of the sewing lines of the pinned squares, chain-piecing the squares together (see the bottom sidebar on facing page).

5 With the wrong side of the marked square up, clip away the extra triangles of both fabrics with scissors to reduce bulk. Leave a ¼" (6 mm) seam allowance. Be careful! Do not cut off the triangle that you just sewed on. Discard the triangles you've removed. Press the triangle open, toward the corner. Repeat with the remaining squares.

6 With the right sides together, pin a remaining fabric C square to the opposite corner of each rectangle. This square will overlap the first triangle. Sew along the stitching line. Cut off the excess and press. Repeat to make four double, half-square triangle units.

7 Arrange the nine units in the sawtooth star design on your work surface or design board.

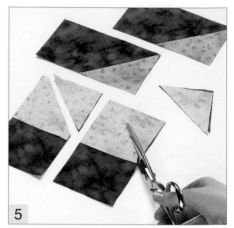

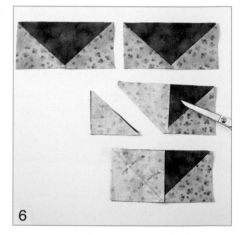

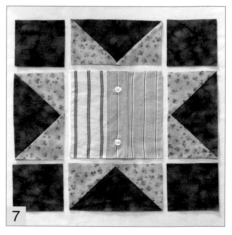

8 Pin and sew the units to form three rows. Remember to pin the units right sides together and to stitch with a ¼" (6 mm) seam allowance. Press the seams in the outer rows in one direction and the seams of the middle row in the opposite direction (page 42).

9 Pin together the first two rows, beginning at the intersection of seams so the edges align. The seam allowances will "butterfly" and lie flat. Sew the seam and press it away from the middle row. Pin and sew to attach the last row. Press the seam away from the middle row.

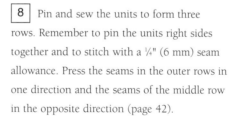

Stitch new buttons on
your finished quilt for fun.

harvesting shirts and blouses

Why part with your favorite garments? To harvest the fabric, first lay the garment flat on the table, front side down. With scissors, cut up the sides of the back, removing the seams. Cut across the yoke just below the seam. Cut off the rolled hem on the bottom.

Now you'll have a big square of fabric. Iron it flat. Decide how much you'll need and put the rest away for future blocks.

If you want to incorporate the front button placket into your block, button the shirt. With the placket centered, rough-cut a square a few inches (centimeters) larger than the square you'll need for your block unit. You can also button the front pieces of two different shirts—as shown here and in the project—before rough-cutting the square.

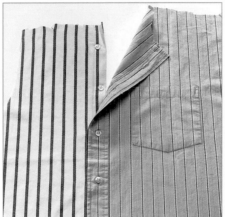

Press and stitch down the button placket, stitching over the garment's topstitching. Be sure the machine foot doesn't hit the buttons. Trim the piece to the cut size: 6½" (16.5 cm) square. Remove any buttons that are near the outside edges of the fabric.

Sew a line of stitching ⅛" (3 mm) around the entire square, to keep layers together. Remove the buttons. After the finished block is sewn into a quilt, and the quilt is stitched, you can add them back.

chain piecing

When sewing a corner, the fabric point can sometimes get pulled into the sewing machine, jamming the fabric. Chain piecing will help you avoid this problem and will make piecing units go much faster, too.

Begin sewing about ¼" (6 mm) from the edge of the fabric. Backstitch to the corner and then continue sewing forward on the sewing line. As you near the opposite corner, slow down and sew off the unit. Do not cut the threads.

Push the next fabric unit close to the end of the first one. Let the feed dogs catch the point and pull it smoothly through the machine. Cut the units apart later.

dress casual quilt

Now that you've made a few blocks, you have most of the skills you need to make an entire quilt. This project will take you from beginning to end. It's a good size for a wall hanging, throw, or crib-size quilt. You'll learn to assemble the quilt top, make the backing, and add a beautiful French binding.

You can make this quilt with any blocks that have a cut size of 12½" (31.5 cm). Combine repeats of the same block style, or two different styles, or create twenty unique blocks. This project has two plain blocks and multiples of the four different blocks you learned how to make in this chapter: Five Easy Pieces, the Bandana Fofanna Nine Patch, the Night-and-Day Pinwheel, and the Button-Down Sawtooth Star.

Project Facts
- **Finished Size:** 48" × 60" (122 × 152.5 cm)

Note: All fabric amounts are based on 42" to 44" (106.5 to 112 cm)-wide quilter's cotton.

Find Your Fabrics
- 20 finished blocks of your choice, each with a cut size of 12½" (31.5 cm) square
- **For Backing:** Cut 3 yd. (2.75 m) of cotton into two 1½ yd. (1.4 m) pieces
- **For Binding:** Cut ½ yd. (0.5 m) of cotton into six strips that measure 2½" (6.5 cm) wide by the width of the fabric
- **For Batting:** Cut a piece at least 52" × 64" (132 × 162.5 cm)

dress casual quilt

The Quilt Top

1 Arrange the blocks in four rows of five blocks each. Lay them on the floor, the bed, or a large work surface—or arrange them on a design board (see page 31). Move the blocks around until you are pleased with the arrangement of colors and patterns.

2 After you have arranged the blocks, number the rows. The numbers will make it easy for you to sew the blocks in sequence.

Write the row number on a small piece of paper and pin the paper to the block—or mark the blocks with flower-head pins (see page 33). Place the numbers in the upper left-hand corner of the block—but not so close to the edge that the numbering will interfere with the seam allowances. Numbering will help keep the rows right side up as you sew them together.

Number the first block in each row. Leave the row markers on until the entire quilt top is sewn together.

3 One row at a time, sew the four blocks together. Remember to use a ¼" (6 mm) seam allowance. After sewing a row, return it to the design wall or its place on the work surface. Do not iron the seams yet.

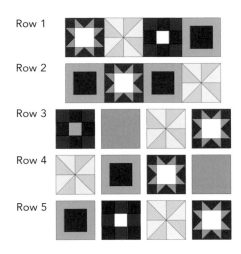

4 When you have sewn all the rows, pick up rows 1, 3, and 5. Press the new seams all in one direction. Return these rows to their position in the design.

5 Next, pick up rows 2 and 4. Press the new seams in the direction opposite from the odd-numbered rows you stitched in step 3.

6 Pick up row 1 and carefully pin it to row 2. Check the markers to be sure the rows will be arranged in the correct direction when they're sewn. Pin at the intersections of the blocks so that the seams butterfly and lie flat (see page 43). Add more pins for security and then sew the seams.

Next, pin and sew row 3 to the row 1 unit (along row 2). You've completed the row 1 unit. Sew together rows 4 and 5 to create the row 4 unit.

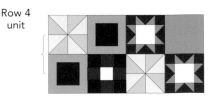

7 Sew the row 1 unit to the row 4 unit. Press all the new seams in one direction—and your quilt top is done!

here's a hint!

You may not be able to finish the quilt top in one sitting. Make a sketch or take a picture of the block arrangement so you can refer to it when you're ready to continue.

The Backing

1 The width of this quilt is wider than the fabric for the back, so you have to piece together the backing fabric. With right sides together, pin and sew the two 1½ yd. (1.4 m) pieces of backing fabric together with a ¼" (6 mm) to ½" (1.3 cm) seam allowance. You will now have one piece that is about 88" × 54" (220 × 137 cm). Slash the selvages every 2" (5 cm) with scissors and press the seam open.

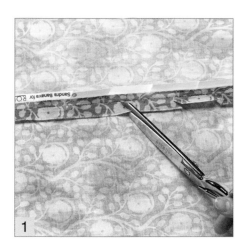

2 Now that you have prepared the quilt top and backing, you are ready to sandwich and stitch the quilt together. Follow the steps on pages 11–15 to assemble your quilt.

The Binding Strip

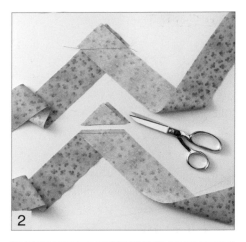

1 After you have stitched the quilt, it's time for the finishing touch—the binding. The quilt binding acts like a tiny frame around the quilt top and provides another design element by adding a bit of color and shape.

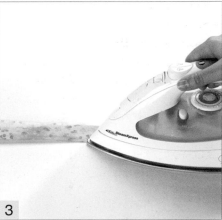

2 Sew the strips' right sides together at right angles to form a continuous strip of binding. Sewing the strips at an angle reduces bulk and makes the binding easier to sew.

Trim off the excess, leaving a ¼" (6 mm) seam allowance. Sew all six strips together, end to end. Press seams to one side. You now have one long strip of binding.

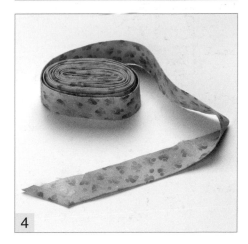

3 Fold the long strip lengthwise, with wrong sides together. Carefully press so that the raw edges meet. Loosely roll the pressed binding strip.

4 Unroll one end of the strip so the binding is flat for several inches (centimeters). Fold the strip's end diagonally toward one lengthwise raw edge. Cut along the fold. Turn the raw edge under ¼" (6 mm) and press.

Refold the end of the binding lengthwise and re-press. You are ready to bind your quilt.

dress casual quilt

Attaching the Binding

1 Lay the stitched quilt sandwich on the work surface and trim the batting and backing an even ¼" (6 mm) wider than the top of the quilt.

2 Begin stitching in the center of one side of the quilt. Lay the binding strip on the quilt top. Line up the raw edges of the binding and the raw edge of the quilt top. Pin down the point of the diagonal.

Before you start, check your even-feed foot to see if it has a marking to guide you. Begin to sew the binding to the quilt about 2" to 3" (5 to 7.5 cm) below the point of the binding. Keep the line of stitching a consistent ¼" (6 mm) away from the edge of the quilt top. You don't have to pin the binding to the quilt top—just sew slowly. Concentrate on keeping the raw edges of the quilt top and binding aligned as you sew.

3 Insert a pin in the binding and quilt top ¼" (6 mm) away from and before the corner. Stitch to the pin. Stop and backstitch. Take the quilt out from under the machine. Remove the pin and cut the threads.

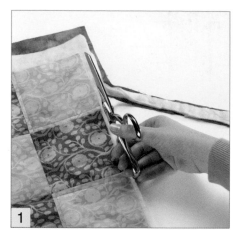

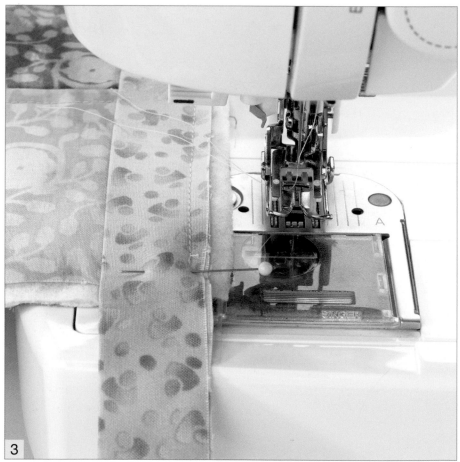

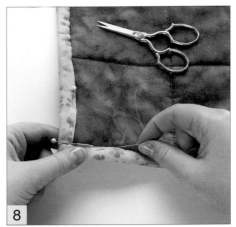

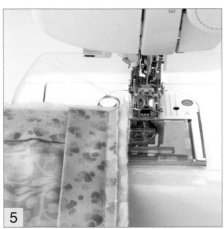

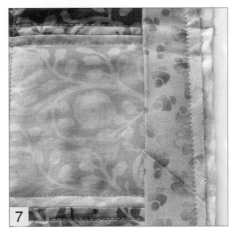

4 Turn the quilt. Fold the binding up at a 45 degree angle.

5 Fold the binding down over the previous fold to cover it. Realign the edges of the binding with the edge of the quilt top. Sew until you are near the next corner. Repeat the last two steps at each corner.

6 Stop sewing when you are about 4" (10 cm) away from the angled opening of the binding. Slip the straight end of the binding into the angled opening. If the binding is too long, trim it straight across so it will fit in the binding.

7 Pin this final part of the binding down. Continue to sew to just beyond the point where the binding began.

8 Fold the binding to the back of the quilt. At the corners, fold the binding to form miters and pin.

9 Hand-sew the binding to the backing. Be careful to catch only the backing and the batting with the needle and thread. Your wonderful quilt is done!

Add your label and start planning another quilt!

foundation piecing

Is there a prom gown or bridesmaid dress lurking in your attic or closet? Or a bag of men's ties you don't want to part with? Any vintage tablecloths or napkins? Deconstruct them and recycle the fabric. The foundation-pieced block projects in this chapter are a great way to turn memories into a quilt.

In foundation piecing, an extra layer supports the block, so it's easy to work with silks and other slippery fabrics. The layer can be either temporary or permanent. The foundation allows for quick, random piecing of blocks and accurate piecing of corners and points.

crazy for you block

Crazy patch is a classic quilt block without any pattern. This Crazy for You Block is made with a "top piecing" technique on a permanent (fabric) foundation. You simply sew randomly arranged fabric pieces to cover a square of muslin. Making a crazy patch is a great way to use up scraps of interesting fabrics—satins, linens, lace, and even fancy embroidered hankies.

Project Facts
- **Cut Size:** 12½" (31.5 cm) square
- **Finished Size:** 12" (30.5 cm) square

Find Your Fabrics
- ½ yd. (0.5 m) muslin
- 12 to 15 fabric scraps, each at least 6" to 10" (15 to 25.5 cm) square

Note: All fabric amounts are based on 42" to 44" (106.5 to 112 cm)-wide quilter's cotton.

Cutting List
- Cut a 13½" (34.5 cm) square from the muslin.

crazy for you block

1 With a pencil, mark a 12½" (31.5 cm) square on the muslin. You can use any type of pencil. This line will not show when the block is finished.

2 Cut a piece of fabric to a shape that is roughly 5" to 6" (12.5 to 15 cm). Trim the shape so it has four or more straight sides. Center this piece, right side up, in the middle of your muslin square. Pin it in place.

3 Cut a straight edge on one side of a second fabric piece. Place that piece right side down on one edge of the first piece, covering the entire edge. Pin and sew a seam ¼" (6 mm) from the raw edges. Stitch through the muslin, too.

4 Flip open the second fabric piece and iron it flat.

5 Continue adding pieces around the first piece. Always add fabrics with the right sides together. After sewing each ¼" (6 mm) seam, flip the work and iron the seam.

You might lose the straight edge and need to piece on top of several fabrics. That's okay as long as every subsequent piece has a straight edge and is large enough to cover the uneven fabric ends.

6 As you add more pieces, work with scissors to trim any excess fabric from the back so that the new pieces will lie flat. Fold the foundation fabric out of the way and trim about ¼" (6 mm) away from the seam. You may have to rip a few stitches from previous seams in order to trim the excess fabric. Be careful not to cut the foundation or the piece you just added.

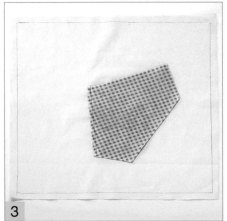

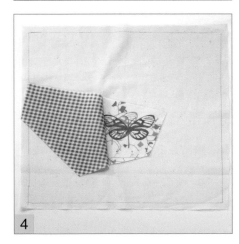

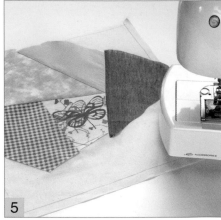

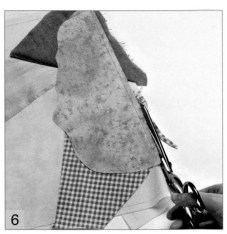

7 Keep adding pieces until the entire block is covered with fabric. You should no longer be able to see the pencil line you drew in step 1. Trim the block to the cut size of 12½" (31.5 cm) square.

8 Traditional crazy patch quilts often have decorative stitching, trims, buttons, or beads in their blocks. These extras are added as a finishing touch, after the blocks are sewn into the quilt and quilted. Consider adding these details as you plan the stitching of your quilt. (The Garden Party Quilt on page 76 has vintage buttons!)

Turn your crazy blocks on end with great buttons or trims!

harvesting fancy dresses

Got an old bridesmaid or prom dress? Let's see what we can do with it. Look it over carefully. Is the fabric clean and in good condition? Check the other criteria for quilt fabrics on pages 18–21, too. If the dress isn't clean, wash or dry-clean it. The label should tell you the correct care requirements and the correct heat setting for pressing.

If the dress has small details, such as bows, straps, or fabric rosettes, you may want to save them to use for embellishments on a finished quilt or other project.

If the dress has an accompanying stole, you might have enough fabric for your quilt project already, without needing to harvest from the dress. If not, focus on the skirt, which will have the most useable fabric. With scissors, remove the bodice—the part of the dress above the waist. (The bodice is usually fitted and shaped, so it may not be usable. If the dress has no waist, cut below the bust darts and curved seams. Cut around the zipper and around buttons, beading, or other hard details.)

Open up the back seam or one side seam of the skirt. Cut away the hem and any lining and interfacings. If the garment has only a few seams, cut them away. If there are a lot of seams, but the fabric lies flat, include the seams in the pieces you cut for your blocks. They will be fairly unnoticeable or, in some cases, might add interesting detail to the block. Press the fabric before cutting units.

peek-a-boo block

In this Peek-a-Boo Block, the foundation fabric "peeks" through to become part of the design itself. The sewing technique is called "sew and flip," and it's just as easy as it sounds. This block is made with beautiful silks harvested from men's neckties, silk brocade fabric, and some scraps of raw silk.

Project Facts
- **Cut Size:** 12½" (31.5 cm) square
- **Finished Size:** 12" (30.5 cm) square

Find Your Fabrics
- **Fabric A:** ½ yd. (0.5 m) or one fat quarter of cotton fabric
- **Fabric Scraps:** 8 to 10 different fabric scraps, at least 14" by 4" (35.5 × 10 cm)
- **Trim:** Flat lace or other trim, at least 18" (45.5 cm) long (optional)

Note: All fabric amounts are based on 42" to 44" (106.5 to 112 cm)-wide quilter's cotton.

Cutting List
- **From Fabric A:**
  Cut a 13½" (34.5 cm) square.
- **From the Fabric Scraps:**
  Cut different-width strips, between 1½" and 3" (4 and 7.5 cm) wide and 14" (35.5 cm) long.

Notions
- chalk marker or chalk pencil
- seam ripper
- featherweight or lightweight fusible interfacing

peek-a-boo block

1 Fold the fabric A square in half diagonally and press. This pressed fold is the centerline. Mark a line 2" (5 cm) away from the centerline on either side with a chalk dispenser or pencil and a ruler.

2 With the right side down, line up the first strip of fabric with one of the marked lines. The edge of the fabric will abut the line, and the bulk of the strip will be in the center of the square. Be sure the strip covers the fabric square at both ends. Pin the fabric in place.

3 Sew the strip to the foundation from one end to the other with a ¼" (6 mm) seam allowance. Flip the fabric to the right side and press it away from the center of the square.

4 Pin the next fabric strip to the unstitched edge of the first strip with right sides together. Sew through all layers with ¼" (6 mm) seam allowances. Flip the work and iron.

5 Continue adding strips until the first side of the square is covered. You can cover the corners with small scraps or squares of fabric. Be sure to cover the block all the way to the edges. Turn the square around and cover the second side to the corner in the same way.

6 When you have finished sewing on the strips, you might want to add a flat piece of lace or crocheted trim down the middle of the foundation fabric that is peeking out—as on the blue fabric in the photo. Pin the trim to the center foldline and sew close to the edge of both sides of the trim.

7 Now trim the block to its cut size, which is 12½" (31.5 cm) square.

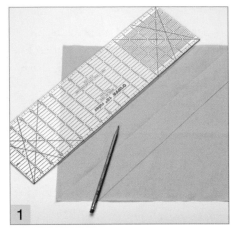

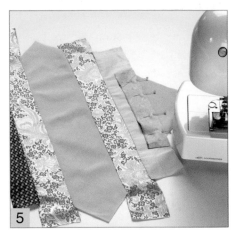

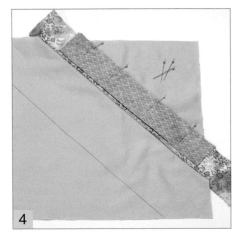

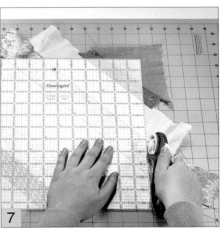

So easy! You've made
another great block!

washing silk neckties

If you're washing just one or two ties, wash them in the sink with a mild soap or shampoo. If you are harvesting a large bunch of ties, wash them in the washing machine.

Sort the light and dark colors. Tie six to eight ties into a loose knot and put them in a small lingerie bag. Wash in cold water with the machine set to a delicate cycle. Remove the ties, untie the knot, and hang them to dry. Then iron them on the wrong side of the fabric with the iron temperature set to silk.

harvesting men's ties

You'll often find men's neckties in memory quilts, which celebrate or remember a special person, but the silky, colorful fabrics are perfect for any quilt or block. Neckties won't provide a lot of fabric, but they are perfect when you need narrow strips.

Check the condition of the tie first. If it is noticeably stained, it's probably not usable. Some stains will wash out; some will become larger with washing. Skip the knit ties and heavy woolen ones, too. Check the label—100 percent silk is the best.

1. Working with the seam ripper, remove the label from the tie. Be careful not to nick the fabric. Clip the thread tacks at either end of the tie.

2. Starting at the wide end of the tie, clip the first couple of stitches that hold the tie closed. Do the same on the narrow end of the tie. Most ties are sewn together by hand, with one long, strong, silk thread. Just grab the thread and pull. The whole seam should come unstitched. (If the tie was constructed in some other way, you might have to use the seam ripper along the length of the tie to open all the stitches.)

3. Open the tie and discard the interfacing. Cut the linings from each end of the tie, but do not unstitch any other seams. Fuse a featherweight or lightweight interfacing to the wrong side of the fabric to add body and make it easier to work with. Fusible interfacing, which bonds with heat, is sold by the yard and also in packages. Follow the product instructions for the correct heat settings for your iron.

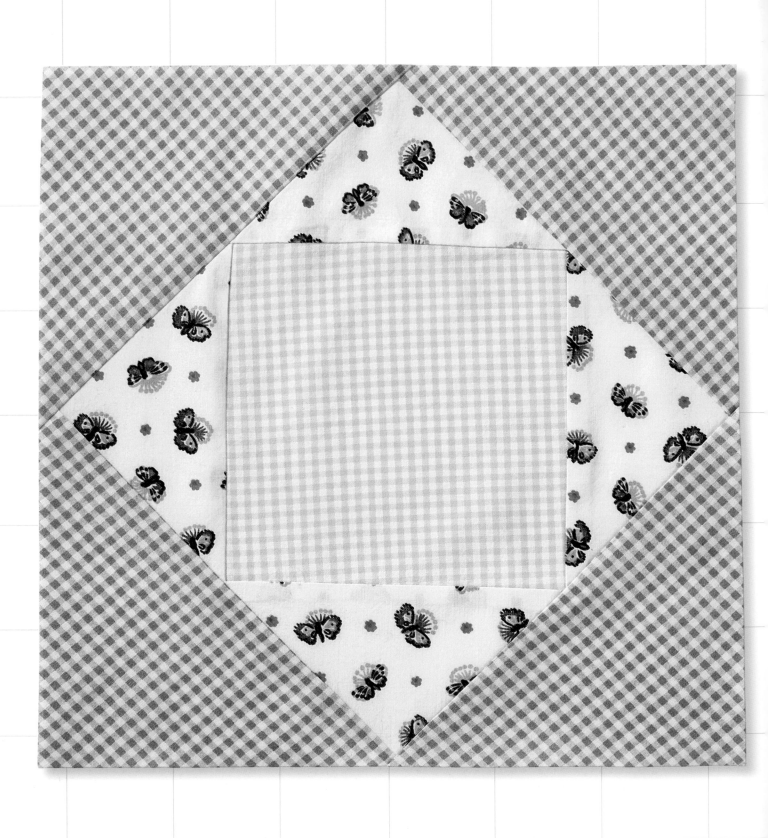

squares without tears block

"Without tears"? Yes! Sewing this block with the underpiecing technique on a temporary foundation makes it trouble free. You'll be amazed at how perfect your squares will be. For the foundation, we used parchment paper (found in the baking aisle at the supermarket). A large piece of tracing paper will also work.

Foundation piecing is great for making corners, too! A vintage 1960s tablecloth gives this block its sweet look.

Project Facts
- **Cut Size:** 12½" (31.5 cm) square
- **Finished Size:** 12" (30.5 cm) square

Find Your Fabrics
- **Fabric A (yellow in photo):** one fat quarter or enough fabric for a 6¾" (17 cm) square
- **Fabric B (butterfly print in photo):** one fat quarter or enough fabric for a 9½" (24 cm) square
- **Fabric C (blue in photo):** one fat quarter or enough fabric for a 12" (30.5 cm) square

Note: All fabric amounts are based on 42" to 44" (106.5 to 112 cm)-wide quilter's cotton.

Notions
- 13½" (34.5 cm) or larger square of parchment, tracing paper, or tear-away stabilizer
- fine-point permanent marker

1 Transfer the dimensions of the block onto your parchment paper square. The template on page 104 will give you the dimensions, and your rulers and the gridded mat will make measuring easy. Work with a fine-tipped permanent marker. (In some of the photographs, the parchment was marked with pencil for greater visibility.) Be precise with your measurements. The lines you draw will be your stitching lines.

2 Add ¼" (6 mm) seam allowances to the outer edges of the 12" (30.5 cm) square. (They are not included in the template dimensions.) It helps to note directly on the pattern where each fabric will go. Then sew on the marked side as you piece the block.

3 Cut a 6¾" (17 cm) square of fabric A. This square will be the center square of the block.

4 From fabric B, cut a 9½" (24 cm) square. Cut this square into quarters by cutting it diagonally twice. From fabric C, cut a 12" (30.5 cm) square. Cut this square in quarters by cutting it diagonally twice.

5 Center the fabric A square right side up on the unmarked side of the paper. Hold everything up to a light or to a window to check that the fabric square covers the center square on the paper.

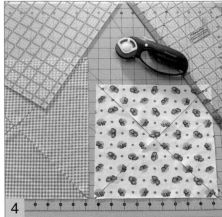

6 Align a fabric B triangle with the top of the fabric A square. Be sure the right sides are together. Both pieces of fabric should be on the unmarked side of the paper. Pin the fabric from underneath, on the marked paper side. Hold everything up to the light to be sure that both fabrics cover the stitching line.

7 Put an open-toe or satin foot on your machine so you can see where you are sewing (see page 27). Sew with the paper side up and the fabric beneath the paper. Sew directly on the lines. (Contrasting thread is used in the photograph for visibility.) Start sewing about ¼" (6 mm) in front of one end of the line and continue sewing about ¼" (6 mm) beyond the other end.

8 Turn to the front of your work and flip the triangle. It should extend to the edge of the square. Place a pin in it to keep it from flopping under the machine.

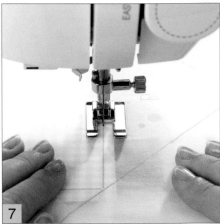

This block looks great when turned on the diagonal.

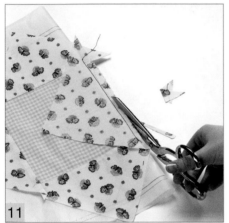

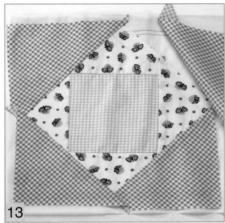

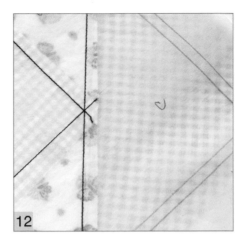

underpiecing

Foundation piecing is extra easy with the underpiecing technique. You'll work with a temporary foundation, such as parchment paper or tear-away stabilizer, which is easy to remove. You can buy tear-away stabilizer in packages, in rolls, or by the yard.

Line up the fabric on one side of the temporary foundation, turn it over, sew along the lines, and move on to the next piece. Then, after the stitching is complete, just tear the foundation away from the back of the fabric. Easy! Once you get the hang of it, you'll be amazed at how perfect your squares will be.

9 | Add the second fabric B triangle opposite the first one. Sew as you did in step 7. Press the triangles away from the center square.

10 | Fold back the triangles and trim ¼" (6 mm) away from the seam and any other excess fabric. Fold the paper back so it does not get in the way (don't cut the paper). Flip back the triangles and pin them in place.

11 | Add the remaining fabric B triangles the same way. Press them open, then flip and trim. Trim across the points to reduce bulk in the corners of your square.

12 | Sew the fabric C triangles the same way. Begin and end the seams ¼" (6 mm) beyond the markings on your paper pattern. Sew right through the intersection of the seams of the fabric B triangles to create a perfect corner.

13 | Add the last triangle and then press the block. Gently tear away the paper from the back.

14 | Trim the block to the cut size of 12½" (31.5 cm) square.

fussy daisies block

The Fussy Daisies Block is a variation on the classic log cabin quilt pattern. In this project, a slippery silk/cotton-blend fabric, a satin harvested from a bridesmaid dress, and a vintage linen napkin combine for a wonderful result. These fabrics could be difficult to piece accurately, but the tear-away foundation and the underpiecing techniques again come to the rescue!

Project Facts
- **Cut Size:** 12½" (31.5 cm) square
- **Finished Size:** 12" (30.5 cm) square

Find Your Fabrics
- **Fabric A:** ¼ yd. (0.25 m) or one fat quarter or enough fabric for four 6½" (16.5 cm) squares
- **Fabric B:** ¼ yd. (0.25 m)
- **Fabric C:** ¼ yd. (0.25 m)

Note: All fabric amounts are based on 42" to 44" (106.5 to 12 cm)-wide quilter's cotton.

Cutting List
Because this block is made with the underpiecing technique (see page 71), fabric amounts are approximate.

If you use fabric scraps, be sure to cut a straight edge on the scrap before you piece it to make it easier to see what you are doing. You'll also need to do less trimming.

- **From Fabric A (for the inside squares):** Cut four 6½" (16.5 cm) squares.
- **From Fabric B and C (for the logs):** Cut 2" (5 cm)-wide strips. Then crosscut to yield eight 8" (20.5 cm)-long strips.

Notions
- tear-away stabilizer, parchment paper, or tracing paper, cut into four 8" (20.5 cm) squares
- fine-point permanent marker

1

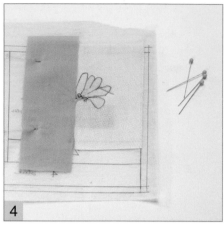

4

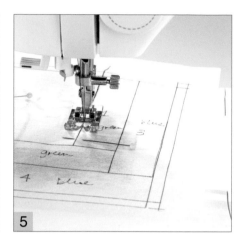

5

7

1 With the marker and a ruler, trace the template on page 105 onto each square of tear-away stabilizer. The traced lines will be the stitching lines, so be as accurate as possible.

Transfer the numbers onto your foundation. They will guide you through the sewing sequence. It's also helpful to note which fabrics you are using, especially if you are going to use alternate colors.

2 Cut squares from fabric A. Cut logs from fabrics B and C.

3 Work on one unit at a time. Put a fabric square right side up on the unmarked side of the foundation. Be sure the fabric covers the lines of the square. Holding the foundation up to a window or a light will help you see.

4 Place the first log (fabric B) right side down on top of the log 1 side of the square. The log will be longer than the square. It should extend past the seam marking and at least ¼" (6 mm) into the log 2 marking.

Flip the log, hold it to the light to check that it is in the proper position, then pin it in place on the marked side of the foundation.

5 Install an open-toe or satin presser foot on your machine (see page 27). You will be sewing directly on the marked lines so the foot will help you see where you are going. (Contrasting thread is used in the photograph for visibility.) Start sewing about ¼" (6 mm) before the ends of the marked lines and stop sewing about ¼" (6 mm) beyond them. Sew on the line between the square and log 1. Press the log away from the square.

6 Flip back the log and, with scissors, trim ¼" (6 mm) away from the seam allowance and also trim any excess fabric. Fold the foundation away so it doesn't interfere—be careful not to cut through it. Flip back the log. Pin it to hold it in place as you sew the next log.

7 Repeat the process to add log 2 (which is also fabric B). Place the log so it extends beyond the seam markings. Pin the log in place on the marked side of the foundation.

Sometimes it really pays to be fussy!

8 Sew on the line between the square and log 2. Press the log, trim it, and pin it to hold it in place as you sew the next log.

9 Repeat the process to add logs 3 and 4 (fabric C).

10 Make another unit exactly like the first one, using fabric B for logs 1 and 2 and fabric C for logs 3 and 4.

11 Reverse the order of the log fabrics to make the remaining two units, using fabric C for logs 1 and 2 and fabric B for logs 3 and 4. The logs will alternate colors in the finished block.

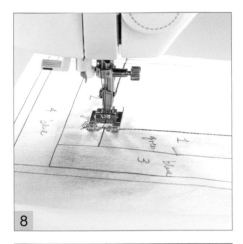

8

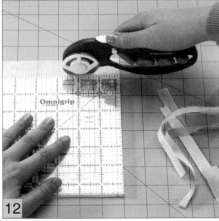

12

12 Press each unit flat and flip it over to the foundation side. With your ruler and rotary cutter, carefully trim along the outer lines on all four sides to make a 6½" (16.5 cm) square.

13 Arrange the blocks on your work surface or design board. Place one square on top of the other, with right sides together. Pin. Repeat with the second set of squares. Sew. Press the new seams in opposite directions.

14 With right sides together, pin at the seam intersections. Sew and press the new seam. Carefully tear off the temporary foundation.

fussy cutting

Quilters do what they call "fussy cutting" when they want to cut out one particular motif in a piece of fabric. Cutting this way is especially useful when working with a one-of-a-kind fabric—for example, vintage linens with a unique pattern or motif, such as the flowers and daisies in this block. Fussy cutting is a quick process, especially with the help of a square ruler that is the same size or larger than the square you want to cut.

Examine the design closely to find areas of the pattern you especially like. Be sure to cut them to the "cut size" dimensions of your block unit. If you want to work with a variety of motifs or several of the same motifs from the fabric, check to be sure there is enough room between the motifs to cut all the pieces you want.

1. Select the motif you want to feature. Center the ruler over the motif. Hold down the ruler firmly as you cut up the right side and across the top. Fussy-cut slightly beyond the size of the square you need.

2. Turn the fabric and align the cut edges with the correct markings on the ruler to get the size you need. Cut the right side and top.

garden party quilt

This beautiful little quilt was made with four foundation blocks in a variety of fabrics harvested from fancy dresses, silk ties, and vintage table linens. Vintage buttons were added after the quilt was stitched. The plain center block and the corners were made from 1960s-era napkins. All the blocks are "set on point," or on the diagonal, to create interest and movement in the design.

Project Facts

The project shown on the facing page is made with a Peek-a-Boo Block, Crazy for You Block, Squares without Tears Block, Fussy Daisies Block, plus one plain block. The photo instruction on the following pages features five Squares without Tears Blocks made in red, white, and blue quilter's cotton and a vintage cotton tablecloth. Fabric amounts are the same for both variations.

- **Finished Size:** 38" (96.5 cm) square

Find Your Fabrics

- Five blocks of your choice, each with a cut size of 12½" (31.5 cm) square
- **For Side and Corner Triangles:** ¾ yd. (0.7 m)
- **For Binding:** ½ yd. (0.5 m)
- **For Backing:** 1¼ yd. (1.15 m)
- **For Batting:** at least 42" (106.5 cm) square

Note: All fabric amounts are based on 42" to 44" (106.7 to 111.8 cm)-wide quilter's cotton.

Cutting List

Cut fabrics for the quilt elements as you are ready to use them. Complete the five blocks before cutting the side and corner triangles.

Cut the backing after you assemble the quilt top. Cut binding strips when you are ready to attach the binding.

- **For Side Triangles:**
  Cut two 13" (33 cm) squares. Crosscut each square on the diagonal once. Each square will give you two side triangles.
- **For Corner Triangles:**
  Cut two 9¼" (23.5 cm) squares. Crosscut them once on the diagonal. Each square will give you two corner triangles.
- **For Binding:**
  Cut four strips that measure 2½" (6.5 cm) wide by the width of the fabric.
- **For Backing:**
  Fabric does not have to be cut or pieced.

garden party quilt

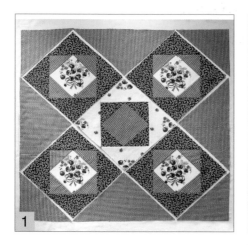

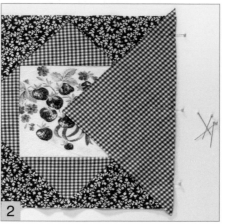

1 Cut the squares for the side and corner triangles. Arrange the five completed blocks and the squares on your work surface or design wall. Mark the rows as top, middle, and bottom, as in the sidebar on the facing page.

2 Begin by making the middle row. Sew the three blocks together with a ¼" (6 mm) seam allowance.

Center a corner triangle at each end, right sides together, and pin. The corners of the triangle might stick out a bit. These pieces of fabric are sometimes called dog ears. Sew. Press all the new seams of this row in one direction.

3 Clip the dog ears of the triangles that stick out of the seam.

4 To make the top row, pin and sew a side triangle to each side of the block. Then press the new seams in the opposite direction of the middle row.

5 Make the bottom row in the same way as you made the top row. Press the new seams in the same direction as the seams in the top row.

6 Now add the corner triangle to the top row. Center the triangle between the seams of the block and pin. Sew. Press the new seam toward the corner and clip any dog ears.

7 Add the last corner triangle to the bottom row. (Be sure that you are adding it on at the bottom and not at the top of the row.) Press the new seam toward the corner and clip any dog ears.

8 Fold the top row over the middle row so the right sides are together. Line up the seams of the middle blocks and pin. The seams should butterfly (see page 43). Then pin across the rest of the block. Sew. Press the new seam toward the top row in the seam line.

9 To make the last seam, fold the bottom row over the middle row, pin at the intersection of the seams, and sew. Press the new seam toward the bottom row. Your quilt top is done!

Liven up other quilt patterns by turning the blocks on their ends!

setting on the diagonal

This project teaches you how to lay out and sew a quilt set on the diagonal. "Set" is a quilter's term that means to position pieces or blocks. The easiest way to understand setting on the diagonal is to simply tilt your head! Look at the photo on page 76 and you see a square quilt. Now tilt your head and imagine the blocks laid out in rows, with a corner on the top and a corner on the bottom. The side and corner triangles fill in the square.

Just like any other quilt, a diagonally set quilt is made up of rows (in this case, three rows). There are two side triangles and one block in the top and bottom rows. There are two corner triangles and three blocks in the middle row. Add a corner triangle to the top and bottom rows and you've set the design on the diagonal!

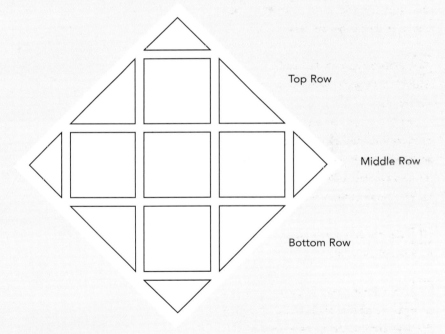

Top Row

Middle Row

Bottom Row

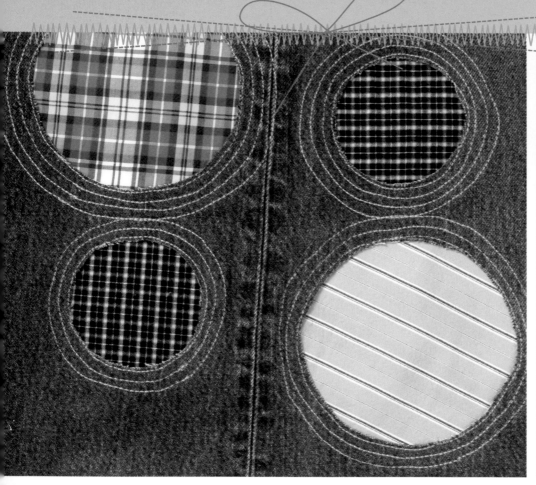

appliqué

When you appliqué, you sew one fabric onto another fabric. Sound simple? Well, it is! This chapter will take you through several different methods of appliqué as you make four one-of-a-kind blocks.

When you're through, you'll have learned all the skills you need to make a sashed and bordered quilt. The Laundry Bag Explosion Quilt (page 100) is a twin-size comforter that lets you turn your collection of favorite T-shirts and jeans into a cool quilt. What a perfect way to recycle clothes! And it makes a great memory keepsake, too. Soon you'll be rummaging around in the laundry bag just to see what else you can quilt!

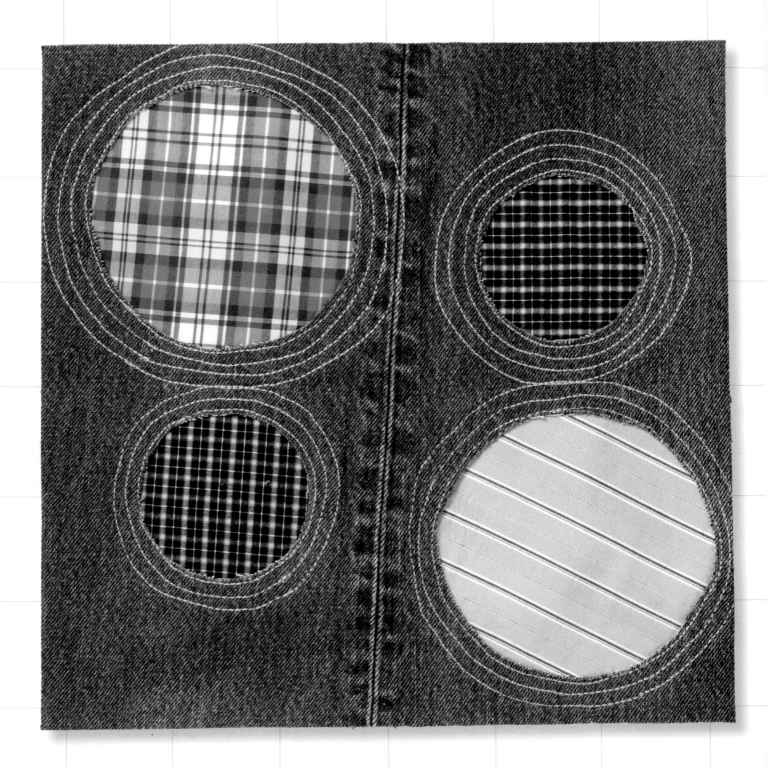

holes-in-your-clothes block

To make this block, you'll need a pair of denim jeans and some fabric scraps. The appliqué edges are unfinished, so they're especially easy to sew—and the denim's natural tendency to fray is a fun design element. Outlining the circles with topstitching adds texture and dimension.

Project Facts
- **Cut Size:** 12½" (31.5 cm) square
- **Finished Size:** 12" (30.5 cm) square

Find Your Fabrics
- One pair of denim jeans (check the label; do not use stretch jeans) or ½ yd. (0.5 m) of lightweight denim or cotton fabric
- One or more scraps of quilter's cotton or harvested cotton shirts or blouses

Cutting List
- Rough-cut a 13" to 14" (33 to 35.5 cm) square of harvested denim.
- Rough-cut several squares of cotton fabric, each several inches (centimeters) larger than the final circle shapes.

Notions
- chalk marker or fabric pencil
- contrasting thread for outline stitching
- lightweight fusible interfacing for circle fabrics
- an old compact disk (CD), protractor, or another circular item less than 5" (12.5 cm) in diameter for tracing

holes-in-your-clothes block

1. On the wrong side of the denim, measure and mark a 12½" (31.5 cm) square with a chalk marker or fabric pencil. Rough-cut the square, leaving an extra inch (2.5 cm) or so all around. You'll trim the block later, after you've finished the appliqué and outline sewing.

2. Working with the CD, protractor, or round object, randomly trace several circles on the fabric. You can make the circles different sizes, but they should not be bigger than 5" (12.5 cm) in diameter. Do not place a circle on a seam and do not overlap the circles.

3. Cut around the markings with scissors and remove the circles. Cut squares of the quilter's cotton or harvested shirt fabric into squares larger than the circular cutouts. If the shirt and blouse fabrics are much lighter weight than the denim fabric, fuse a square of interfacing onto the wrong side of the squares for stability. (Follow the manufacturer's instructions on the package.)

4. With the denim block right side up, slip the squares of fabric under the circles until you are happy with the look of your block. Pin the fabric under the circles one at a time. Be sure each square of fabric is centered and smooth under the circular cutouts.

here's a hint!

To sew evenly around the curve of a circle, stop sewing with the needle in the fabric. (Use the needle-down feature, or turn the hand wheel.) Lift the presser foot, turn the fabric slightly, lower the presser foot, and continue sewing. Repeat as needed.

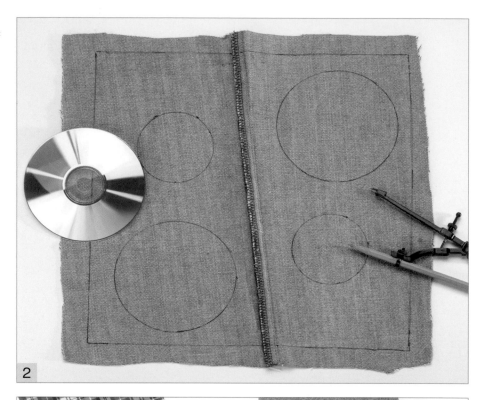

harvesting jeans

Jeans have plenty of seams and details, both for durability and design. Some seams are even double-turned and stitched for strength—for example, the inner leg seam. Try not to include too many of these details in your block. If you do include a seam, choose the flattest seam of the jean legs. A double-stitched seam will be too difficult to sew and too heavy for your block and your quilt.

1. Cut across the jeans, below the front and back pockets. Avoid the zipper and any rivets or metal pieces.

2. Cut along the heavier seam with scissors to open up the pants leg. Lay the pants leg flat. Trim off the hem and heavy seam. Press the harvested fabric if it is wrinkled.

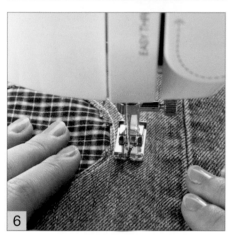

5 | Sew around and close to the edge of each circular opening with contrasting color thread. Backstitch at the beginning and end.

6 | After you have sewn around all the circular openings once, outline them with more stitching. Place the edge of the foot next to the first line of sewing and use the edge as a guide as you sew. Outline-stitch one, two, or three more rows around your circles. Turn over the block and trim off any excess circle fabric.

7 | Trim block to a 12½" (31.5 cm) square.

Who knew holes in clothes could be fun?

brand-new underwear block

Don't worry. You won't have to rummage through your lingerie to make this block. Instead, you'll be shopping for fun prints and novelty fabrics. To make the Brand-New Underwear Block, you'll work with the raw-edge appliqué technique. Then you'll add a bold and colorful finish to the appliqué with an outline of machine satin stitching.

Project Facts
- **Cut Size:** 12½" (31.5 cm) square
- **Finished Size:** 12" (30.5 cm) square

Find Your Fabrics
- **Fabric A (blue solid background in photo):** one fat quarter or ½ yd. (0.5 m)
- **Fabric B (black and white dot in photo):** scrap of quilter's cotton, at least 4" × 10" (10 × 25.5 cm)
- **Fabric C (red dot in photo):** scrap of quilter's cotton, at least 3" × 9" (7.5 × 23 cm)
- **Fabric D (dice print in photo):** ¼ yd. (0.25 m) or one fat quarter of quilter's cotton

Note: All fabric amounts are based on 42" to 44" (106.5 to 112 cm)-wide quilter's cotton.

Cutting List
- Rough-cut a square at least 13" (33 cm) of fabric A.

Notions
- ½ yd. (0.5 m) of double-sided fusible web
- ½ yd. (0.5 m) of tear-away stabilizer
- coordinating thread for satin stitching
- open-toe, satin, or universal presser foot

brand-new underwear block

1 Cut pieces of fusible web that are slightly larger than each of the five appliqué templates (see pages 106–108). With the paper side up, trace each template onto the fusible web. (If both sides of the web have paper backing, refer to the manufacturer's instructions to find the correct side for tracing.) The web bonds the appliqué fabrics to the background fabric, so you don't have to worry about pins or shifting fabrics as you sew.

2 Iron the appliqué fabric so that it is wrinkle free. Place the traced design, fusible side down, on the wrong side of the appliqué fabric. Fuse the web to the fabric. Follow the product instructions for the correct heat settings.

3 Cut out the designs with scissors. Carefully remove the paper backing.

4 Position the appliqué pieces, right side up, on the right side of the background block. Start with the two big pieces, fit them together, and fuse them to the background fabric with the iron. Fit and fuse the smaller pieces until your appliqué is complete.

5 Satin-stitch all the raw edges of the appliqué. Let the machine work at its own pace. Don't push or pull the fabric while you are stitching—just guide it.

It's a good idea to check the length and width of your sitches by making a practice appliqué. You'll also find out if your fabric needs a tear-away stabilizer.

6 If you used a tear-away stabilizer, flip over the block and gently rip away the excess.

7 Trim your block to the cut size of 12½" (31.5 cm) square.

making a practice appliqué

Before you work on your block, take a few minutes to perfect your stitch. Make a little practice appliqué by fusing a couple of pieces of fabric onto a piece of background scrap fabric.

The satin stitch can be adjusted to the width that works best for your project. Because the stitches are often dense, the fabric can pucker and distort. Tear-away stabilizers will help. Cut a piece that is the size of the area to be stitched and place it between the background fabric and the machine. The stabilizer supports the fabric and helps your work slide easily under the needle. When you've finished your appliqué, just tear away the stabilizer from the stitches. It's okay if some remains in the stitches—it won't show in or affect your finished block.

satin-stitch secrets

Practice your satin stitch on scrap fabric before you begin stitching your block. Notice the right and left swings of the needle. You want to be sure that the right swing of the needle goes into the background fabric, quite close to the edge of the appliqué. To make a wider or narrower zigzag, adjust the stitch width selector.

If you want denser satin stitching, shorten the stitch length with the stitch length selector on your machine. If the stitches don't progress easily and seem to get stuck in one place, lengthen the stitch slightly.

Keep your eyes on the edge of the appliqué—not the needle—as you guide your fabric through the machine. If you need to stop sewing with the swing of the needle in a specific position, use the hand wheel.

When two appliqué pieces are placed next to each other, stitch so that the swing of the needle catches both raw edges. Center the two appliqués under the foot. As you guide your fabric, watch the line that forms where both pieces meet.

When you come to a curve, slow down and stitch until you need to turn the fabric to continue. Stop with the needle down on the right swing of the stitch. Lift the presser foot and turn the fabric slightly toward the curve. Lower the presser foot and continue sewing a few stitches. Repeat these steps as needed to satin-stitch smoothly around the entire curve.

To satin-stitch around a corner, stitch to the end of the edge. Stop with the needle down on the right swing of the stitch. Lift the presser foot and pivot the fabric. Lower the presser foot and begin stitching again. The stitches will overlap and make a perfect corner.

Satin stitches make a great-looking finish!

all my favorite t-shirts block

Everyone has favorite T-shirts that just can't be worn anymore—but can't be parted with, either! Why not turn them into quilt blocks to give them new and useful lives! A large, printed design makes a great plain block by itself. Learn some quick appliqué tricks, and you can add small insignias, logos, or other images to your block, too.

Project Facts
- **Cut Size:** 12½" (31.5 cm) square
- **Finished Size:** 12" (30.5 cm) square

Find Your Fabrics
- One T-shirt for background, large enough so you can cut a 14" (35.5 cm) square
- One or more T-shirts with small designs for appliqués

Notions
- ¾ yd. (0.7 m) nonwoven, lightweight, fusible interfacing
- ½ yd. (0.5 m) tulle (fine nylon netting)

all my favorite t-shirts block

1 Plan the layout of your design, allowing for any small appliqués. Launder the T-shirts before you begin—but avoid fabric softeners, which will prevent the fusible interfacing from adhering later.

2 Cut the T-shirt up the sides and across the top for the background portion of the block. Lay the fabric on the work surface and rough-cut the area around the design so that it is at least 14" (35.5 cm) square.

Always rough-cut T-shirt pieces larger than you need them to be. This way, when you cut the piece to size later, you can be sure the stabilizer is fused all the way to the outer edges, which will keep the piece from raveling or curling.

3 T-shirts are made from stretchy knits, so you need to back them with fusible interfacing. The extra weight and stability will help you cut and piece accurately. Cut a piece of fusible interfacing the same size as the rough-cut T-shirt. With the wrong sides together and the printed side facedown, fuse the interfacing to the block with the iron, working with a damp press cloth on top of the interfacing.

4 Rough-cut the shaped appliqués the same way you did the background portion, at least 2" (5 cm) larger than the design.

5 Before fusing the interfacing to the appliqué shapes, trim the interfacing so it is about ½" (1.3 cm) smaller on each side. Fuse as in step 3. With the right side of the appliqué facedown, turn up ½" (1.3 cm) on each side and press, with a damp press cloth between the interfacing and the iron. (If you are working with circular or curved shapes, see the sidebar on the facing page.)

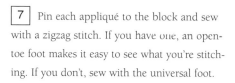

6 Position all the appliqués to make sure they will fit within the finished 12" (30.5 cm) square block. You need only a few pins to hold down the edges.

7 Pin each appliqué to the block and sew with a zigzag stitch. If you have one, an open-toe foot makes it easy to see what you're stitching. If you don't, sew with the universal foot.

8 Start sewing with the right swing of the needle just at the outside edge of the appliqué. This will keep the thread just on the edge of the appliqué, so you won't see the thread color on the block fabric (contrasting thread was used here for visibility).

9 Stop at the corner with the needle down on the right swing. Raise the presser foot, pivot the fabric, and continue sewing. Remember to backstitch at the beginning and end of the stitching. (For tips on stitching curves and corners, see page 89.)

10 After you've sewn all the appliqués, trim the block to its cut size of 12½" (31.5 cm). Never iron directly on the surface of the printed design. Press with design side down or with a damp press cloth or parchment paper.

working with curved shapes

Turning under the raw edges of circular and curved appliqué shapes is a little tricky—but here's an easy way to get smooth, even edges. You'll need some tulle, a very fine, lightweight nylon netting, also known as "illusion."

1. Rough-cut the T-shirt design into a square shape, allowing for at least 2" (5 cm) more than the desired finished size on all sides. Cut a piece of fusible interfacing the same size as the square. With wrong sides together and working with a press cloth, fuse the interfacing to the square.

2. With a chalk marker or fabric pencil, draw a circle around the design. (It helps to work with a compass or to trace around a glass or bowl.) The circle should be the same size as the desired finished size of the appliqué.

3. Cut a piece of tulle the same size as the rough-cut square. Pin it to the right side of the appliqué.

4. Set your machine to very small stitches and sew along the drawn line, completely around the circle. Both the design and the traced line will be visible through the tulle.

5. Carefully make a small slit in the middle of the tulle. Then trim about ⅛" (3 mm) from the stitched circle.

6. Carefully turn the circle right side out through the slit in the tulle and push out the seam. With your fingers, flatten the seam allowance under the tulle. Press with a damp press cloth.

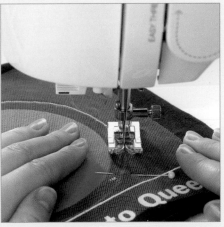

7. The circle now has a perfect finished edge and is ready to appliqué to your block.

Cozy up under a quilt made entirely of favorite T-shirt blocks!

in-my-pocket block

Do you have sports tickets, movie stubs, and bits and pieces of paper with sentimental value? Here's a fun and easy way to turn them into a special block! All you need is a pocket T-shirt, a sheet of printable paper-backed fabric, and a handful of memorabilia to print. You'll create turned-edge appliqué with invisible thread to create the illusion of real paper items in the pocket.

Project Facts
- **Cut Size:** 12½" (31.5 cm) square
- **Finished Size:** 12" (30.5 cm) square

Find Your Fabrics
- One T-shirt with pocket
- Nonwoven, lightweight, fusible interfacing, at least 14" (35.5 cm) square

Notions and Materials
- sew-in, cotton, printable paper-backed fabric
- small paper memorabilia
- invisible thread
- press cloth

1 Position the pocket slightly off center and rough-cut the T-shirt into a 14" (35.5 cm) square. Be sure to leave enough room over the pocket to place an appliqué.

2 Fuse the square of fusible interfacing onto the back of the rough-cut square. Work with a press cloth to protect your iron.

3 Create your printed fabric appliqué, following the steps in the sidebar on facing page.

4 Cut around the printed image, leaving ¼" to ⅜" (6 to 1 cm) of fabric around the edges of the appliqué. Clip into any corners.

5 Fold and press the raw edges to the back. Don't bother folding the bottom edge—it won't be visible.

6 Slip the appliqué into the pocket to test how it fits. Trim the fabric at the bottom of the appliqué as needed so there isn't a lot of bulk in the pocket. Pin the appliqué into the pocket of the shirt.

7 With invisible thread and an open-toe or universal presser foot on your machine, carefully zigzag-stitch the appliqué in place. As you approach the corner, you'll want to use the needle down control if you have one. If your machine doesn't have a needle-down control, you'll need to slow the machine as you approach the corner. Stop a short distance before the corner and turn the hand wheel to position the needle in the corner of the fabric. Then raise the presser foot, turn the fabric, lower the presser foot, and continue sewing. Remember to backstitch at the beginning and end of each line of stitching.

5

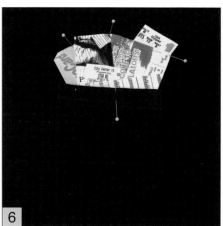

6

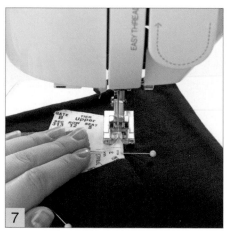

7

8 Close the pocket with a line of stitching.

9 Trim your In-My-Pocket Block to the cut size of 12½" (31.5 cm) square.

printing on fabric

You can print onto fabric anything that you can run through your printer or copier. All you need is a sheet or package of sew-in, cotton, paper-backed printable fabric, which you can find in a fabric or crafts store. Choose a product that is washable and colorfast. The sheets fit right into the paper tray of your machine.

Search through your stash of memorabilia—photos, ticket stubs, programs, etc.—and select a group of small items that will fit inside the T-shirt pocket. Slip them into the pocket and arrange them as you wish. Try to make the edges as straight as possible,

because after you copy the pieces onto fabric, you'll turn under and appliqué the straight edges.

Secure the items together with glue or paper clips. Place the grouping in the center of the copy machine or printer bed. Cover it with a piece of plain white paper to provide a backing and close the lid.

Always check your image by printing on paper first. When you are happy with the way the grouping looks on paper, load the paper-backed printable fabric and print. Some products will need to be rinsed or ironed to remove excess ink. Follow the manufacturer's instructions.

Now you know what to do with all
those pieces of paper you save!

laundry bag explosion quilt

Here's one way to get that laundry off the floor! Make this twin-size comforter quilt. This project contains a plain T-shirt block and multiples of the appliqué blocks you've learned in this chapter. The blocks are arranged in three rows of four blocks each. The sashing and sashing border highlight each one-of-a-kind block. Add a wide border to create an overall frame. The final touch is a bright binding.

Project Facts

The project shown on the facing page and in the diagram on page 100 is made with twelve blocks. The photo instruction features a small quilt top made with nine blocks. The process of sashing and attaching a border is always the same no matter how many blocks are in the quilt top.

- **Finished Size:** 68" × 84" (172.5 × 210 cm)

Find Your Fabrics

- Twelve blocks of your choice, each with a cut size of 12½" (31.5 cm) square
- **Fabric A (sashing and sashing border):** 2 yd. (1.8 m)
- **Fabric B (wide border):** 2 yd. (1.8 m)
- **Fabric C (binding):** ¾ yd. (0.7 m)
- **For Backing:** 5 yd. (4.5 m)
- **For Batting:** at least 72" × 88" (183 × 224 cm)

Cutting List

- **From Fabric A:**
  Cut fifteen strips that measure 4½" (11.5 cm) wide by the width of the fabric.
- **From Fabric B:**
  Cut seven strips that measure 8½" (21.5 cm) wide by the width of the fabric.
- **From Fabric C:**
  Cut eight strips that measure 2½" (6.5 cm) wide by the width of the fabric.
- **For Backing:**
  Cut into two 2½ yd. (2.5 m) pieces.

Note: The width and length of the elements of this quilt are wider than the width of the fabric. You will need to piece together some of the sashing borders and border strips before cutting and pinning them to the quilt top.

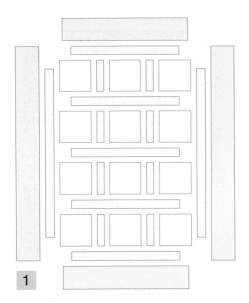

1

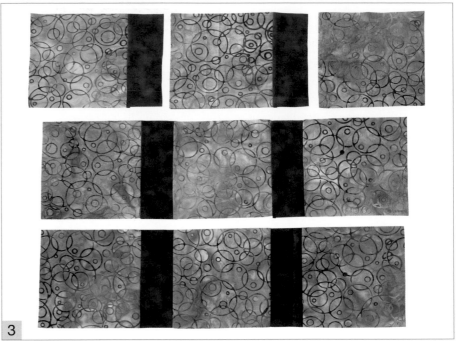

3

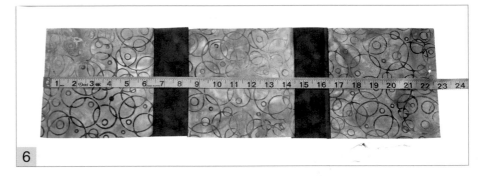

6

1 For the Laundry Bag Explosion Quilt, lay the twelve blocks on your work surface or design board and rearrange them until you are happy with their placement. To help you remember the block arrangement as you sew, take a photograph or make a sketch of the layout—or number the rows with paper or pins (page 33).

2 Cut the strips for the sashing, then cross-cut the short vertical sashing strips. The lengths should be equal to the cut size of the block. For the Laundry Bag Explosion Quilt, the strips would be 12½" (31.5 cm) long.

3 Connect the sashing to your blocks in this order. Start by connecting blocks with short, vertical sashing strips to form the rows.

4 Pin and sew the sashing strips to the blocks of each row. Remember to use a ¼" (6 mm) seam allowance. Sew one block at a time. Do not sew sashing strips to the ends of the row. The sashing border, added later, will provide the sashing for this area.

5 Continue pinning and sewing blocks and sashing together to make each row. Press the seams toward the sashing.

6 After you have assembled the rows of the blocks, you will connect them with horizontal sashing strips.

Measure across the center of a row with a tape measure to determine the correct cut length for these strips. Cut every horizontal sashing strip to this length. (Remember, you might have to piece your strips to get the length you need.)

7 Lay out the rows on the work surface or design board. Refer to your photo or sketch to check the order and orientation of the rows.

8 Pin and sew the horizontal strips to the bottom of each row. Sew the final horizontal strip to the top of the top row. Pin and sew the rows together until you have one large piece. Press the new seams toward the sashing.

9 To complete the sashing border, you'll add a long vertical strip to each side. To determine the cut length of these two vertical sashing strips, measure vertically down the center of the quilt. Cut both strips this length. Pin and sew each vertical sashing border strip to the sides.

10 The wide borders are attached in the same way as sashing borders. Measure the width of the quilt across the center to determine the cut size of the top and bottom borders. (Remember, you might have to piece your strips to get the length you need.) Cut, pin, and sew these borders to your quilt top.

11 Next, measure the length of the quilt down the center to determine the cut size of the vertical side borders. Cut, pin, and sew these borders to your quilt top. The quilt top is done!

12 The top of the Laundry Bag Explosion Quilt is wider than the width of the backing fabric, so you need to piece together the back. With right sides together, pin and sew the two 2½ yd. (2.5 m) pieces of backing together at the selvage edge to form a single piece that is about 88" × 90" (224 × 229 cm).

13 With scissors, cut into the selvages every 2" (5 cm) and press open the seam. When sandwiching this quilt, position the seam so it runs vertically down the center.

14 Now that the quilt top and backing are prepared, sandwich and stitch the quilt together. (Or, you can send it to a professional long-arm quilter for sandwiching, stitching, and finishing.)

15 Cut the binding strips and bind the finished quilt (pages 56–57)

here's a hint!

When sewing sashing strips and borders, always pin and sew with the smaller piece on top. Pin from the center of the strip toward each end, placing pins 4" to 6" (10 to 15 cm) apart. The strip will lie evenly over the larger piece, without shifting or puckering.

Your laundry never looked so good!

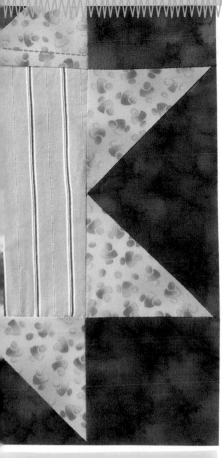

templates

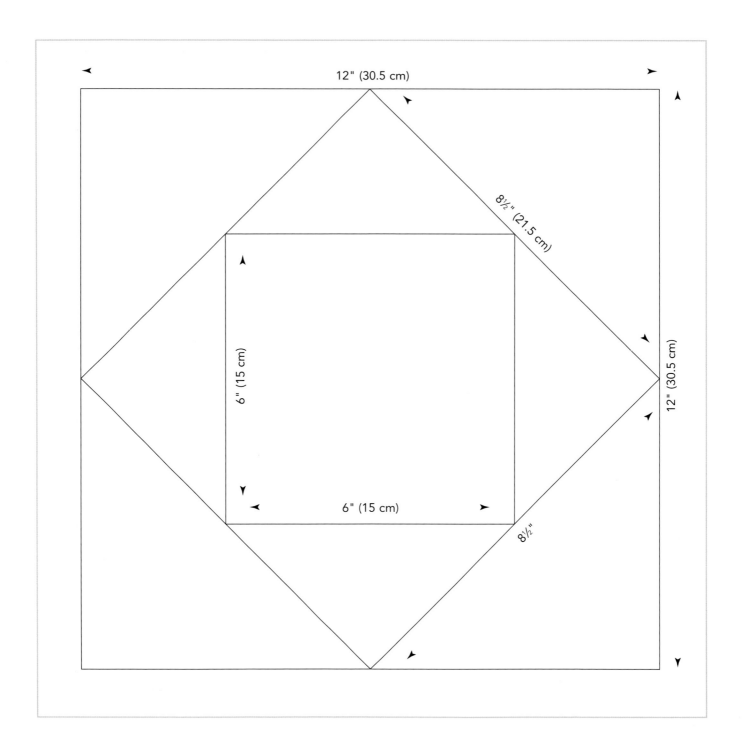

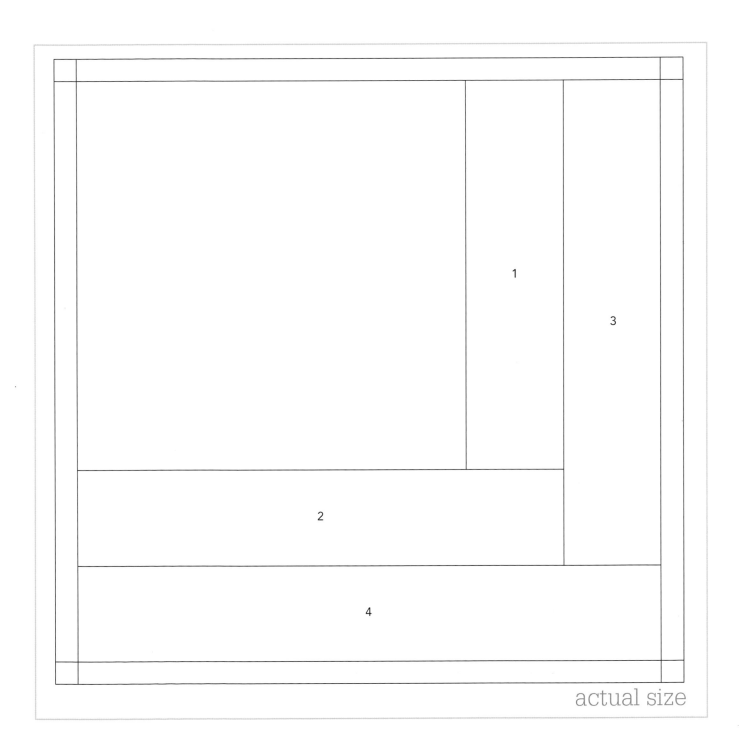

actual size

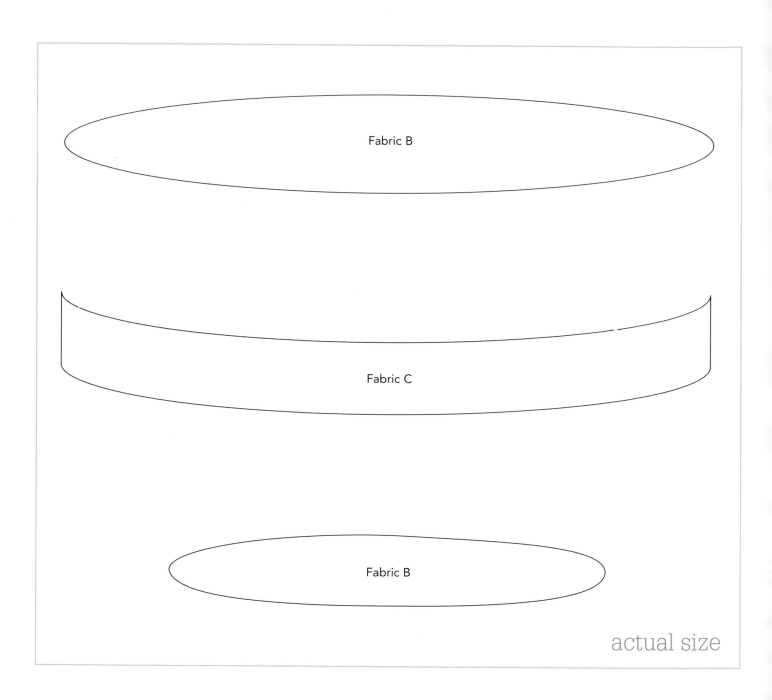

Fabric B

Fabric C

Fabric B

actual size

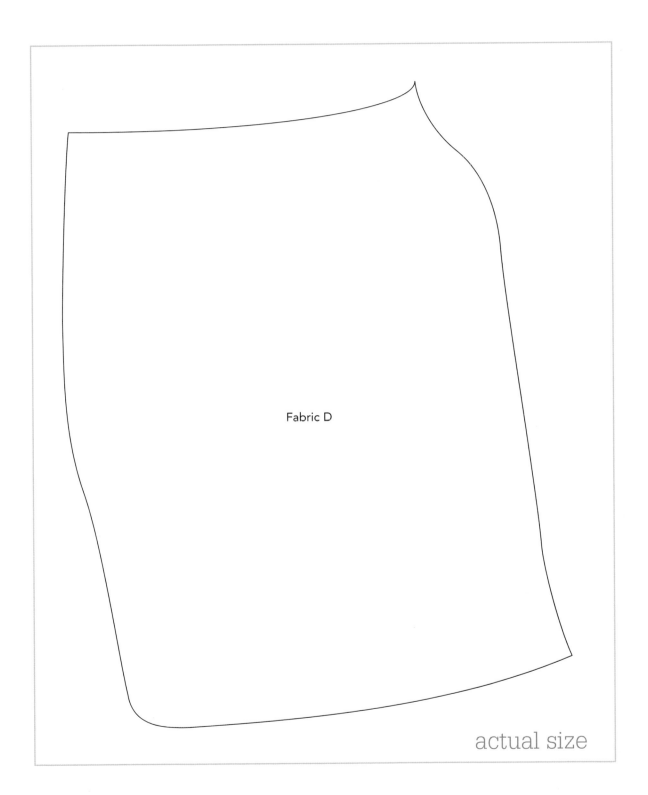

Fabric D

actual size

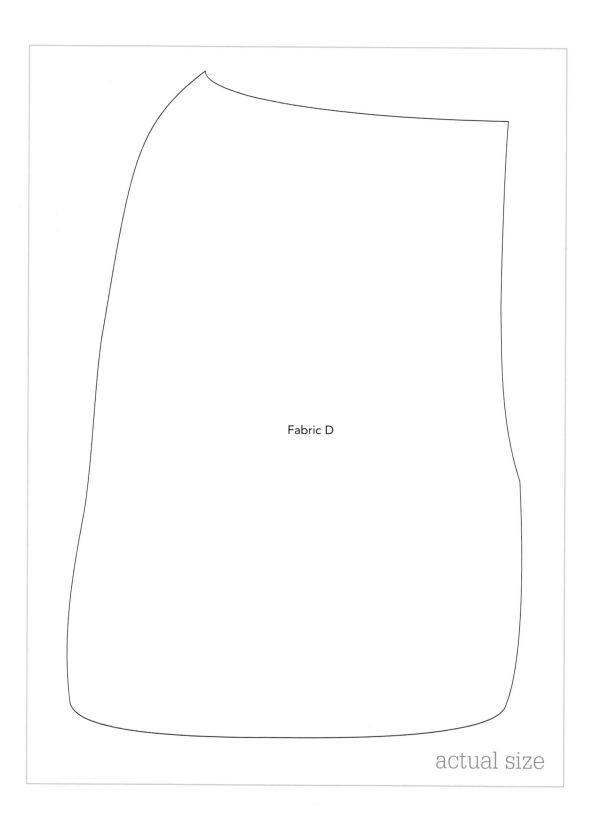

Fabric D

actual size

suppliers

Buttons
JHB International Inc.
1955 S. Quince Street
Denver, CO 80231
303-751-8100
www.buttons.com

Fabric
Robert Kaufman Fabrics
Box 59266, Greenmead Station
Los Angeles, CA 90059
800-877-2066
www.robertkaufman.com

Quilting Services
Little Red Quilt House
60 Access Road
Stratford, CT 06615
203-258-9464
www.lrqh.com

Sewing Machine and Accessories
Singer Sewing Company
1224 Heil Quaker Boulevard
PO Box 7017
LaVergne, TN 37086
800-474-6437
www.singerco.com

T-Shirts
NYC Subway Line
www.nycsubwayline.com

No One and the Somebodies
www.noats.com

Big Melon Gear Inc.
www.bigmelongear.com

Vintage Linens, Trim, and Buttons
Dusty's Vintage Textiles
150 Stafford Road
Holland, MA 01521
413-245-0339

Creative Publishing international

Copyright © 2008 Catherine J. Perri

First published in the United States of America by Creative Publishing international, Inc., a member of Quayside Publishing Group
400 First Avenue North, Suite 300
Minneapolis, MN 55401
1-800-328-3895
www.creativepub.com

ISBN-13: 978-1-58923-390-4
ISBN-10: 978-1-58923-390-5

p. 110, CIP data:

Library of Congress Cataloging-in-Publication Data

Perri, Kate, 1952-
  Quilt blocks and quilts from your favorite fabrics : Recycling fabrics as you learn to quilt / Kate Perri.
      p. cm. --
  Includes index.
  ISBN-13: 978-1-58923-390-4
  ISBN-10: 1-58923-390-5
  1. Quilting--Patterns. 2. Patchwork--Patterns. 3. Appliqué--Patterns. I. Title. II. Series.

  TT835.P4491125 2008
  746.46'041--dc22

                                    2008014585

Technical Editor: Beth Baumgartel
Copy Editor: Carol Polakowski
Proofreader: Alissa Randa Cyphers
Page Layout: Megan Cooney

Printed in Singapore by Star Standard Industries (Pte) Ltd

acknowledgments

Love and thanks to Aron, Dan, and Ben. I simply couldn't do it without your love and support. (Sorry about the mysterious disappearing laundry.)

As always, my thanks to Susan Guagliumi for years of friendship. Thanks to Nancy Rosenberger for her generosity and for the Quilt Cottage. Thank you to Madalyn Romano for support and laughs, and to Lisa Ihde Costa for dropping everything to come see what's on my wall no matter how cattywampus things may be. Thank you, Lori Christian, for laundry tips for vintage fabrics. Thank you, Deb Cannarella, Beth Baumgartel, and everyone at Creative Publishing international.

My thanks to so many friends and students, too numerous to list, for piles of ties, jeans, T-shirts, fancy dresses, and priceless ticket stubs, and for sharing my excitement and laughing at my jokes.

Without great fabrics and trims, it wouldn't be so much fun to sew. Thank you to Emmie Goldenbaum and Frank Cappiello at Robert Kaufman for the wonderful fabric. Thanks to Michele Piccolo of Dusty's for fabulous vintage. Thanks to Janice and Mark Roy and Kelly Mitchell of Little Red Quilt House for beautiful work and for always coming through for me. Thank you, Lynne Lambert, the Meiningers, the Yankou brothers, and the MTA for the great T-shirts.

about the author

Kate Perri loves to quilt, sew, and knit. She has made hundreds of custom quilts with new and vintage materials, photographs, and paper memorabilia. Kate also finds great joy in introducing teens and adults to the sewing machine and helping them create all sorts of projects. She teaches private classes and workshops and in after- school and camp programs. Kate is also the author of *Easy Singer Style: Fashions & Accessories* (Creative Publishing international, 2007). Visit her at www.kateperridesigns.com.

also available

Easy SINGER Style
Pattern-free Fashion & Accessories
ISBN: 978-1-58923-312-6

Easy SINGER Style
Pattern-free Home Accents
ISBN: 978-158923-320-1

Easy SINGER Style
Quick and Easy Window Treatments
ISBN: 978-1-58923-351-5

Easy SINGER Style
Quick and Easy Sewing with your Serger
ISBN: 978-1-58923-350-8

SINGER Simple Sewing Guide
ISBN: 978-1-58923-313-3

SINGER Simple Home Décor Handbook
ISBN: 978-1-58923-314-0

SINGER Simple Mending and Repair
ISBN: 978-1-58923-340-9

SINGER Simple Decorative Machine Stitching
ISBN: 978-1-58923-341-6